W9-DAY-133

Taverns and Stagecoaches

of

New England

VOLUME II

Presenting

*more facts and interesting comments on the era of stage-
coach service over rough and bumpy highways when the
hospitable taverns were welcome havens for weary travelers
at the end of the day's journey.*

By
ALLAN FORBES
and
RALPH M. EASTMAN

Printed for the
STATE STREET TRUST COMPANY
BOSTON
1954

Copyright 1954

by the

STATE STREET TRUST COMPANY

Boston

THE RAND PRESS

Boston

FOREWORD

The reception given our first volume on this same subject last year was most gratifying and many helpful suggestions were sent us about old taverns for inclusion in this year's brochure. Unfortunately, space does not allow us to mention all of these and we hope, therefore, for sympathetic understanding of our problem of selection which inevitably means that some of the suggestions could not be carried out. They are, nevertheless, very much appreciated.

We hope that in these two volumes we have been able to indicate to our readers the important part filled by the stage-coaches and taverns in the development of transportation services to meet the needs of industry and commerce in the early days of our country. While outmoded years ago, in their time they did much to expedite the expansion of this great nation and they merit the respect and appreciation of us all for the major role they played.

Acknowledgments

As usual, in the preparation of our publications, we received the ready cooperation of James L. Bruce of the Bostonian Society; of members of the staff of the Boston Public Library and of Dennis A. Dooley, State Librarian and his associates. We also desire to give public recognition to the following members of our staff: Miss Alice G. Higgins for her assistance in research, Miss Katherine G. Rogers, Miss Alita Gray, Miss Helen Williamsen and Miss Marion Lawless for their work in typing the manuscript and the correspondence necessary in the compilation of this brochure.

We found the following publications very helpful as sources of material, and appreciate the cooperation of the publishers and authors in granting us permission to use excerpts from them: *Coaching Days and Coaching Ways*, by W. O. Tristram, courtesy of MacMillan & Company Ltd., London; *The Colonial Tavern*, by Edward Field, published by Preston and Rounds; *From the Stagecoach to the Railroad Train and Street Car*, by G. Glover Crocker; *The Great White Hills of New Hampshire*, by Ernest Poole, Doubleday & Co., Inc., publishers; *Highway Practice in the United States of America*, published in 1949 by the U.S. Public Roads Administration; *History of the Town of Canton*, by Daniel V. T. Huntoon; *The Nancy Flyer*, by Ernest Poole, Thomas Y. Crowell Co., publishers; *Old Boston Taverns and Tavern Clubs*, by Samuel Adams Drake, with additional material by Walter Kendall Watkins; *Old New England Inns*, by Mary Caroline Crawford, L. C. Page & Co., publishers; *Stage-Coach and Tavern Days*, by Alice Morse Earle; *The Story of Walpole*, 1724–1924, by Willard de Lue, well-known feature story writer of the *Boston Globe* and *The Turnpikes of New England*, by Frederic J. Wood, (now out of print) considered the first exhaustive and authoritative work on this subject. We recommend these and others mentioned in our brochure to those who wish to pursue the study of the interesting events of stagecoach and tavern days. We are grateful to Mrs. Grace Goulder Izant and to The World Publishing Company, Cleveland and New York, for permission to use in our story of the *Bunch of Grapes* material about the Ohio Company taken from the very interesting book *This Is Ohio* written by Mrs. Izant and published during the Ohio Sesquicentennial Year, 1953. Also, we found helpful in checking data the *American Guide Series* written by the Federal Writers Project of the Works Progress Administration of the various New England States, published by Houghton Mifflin & Co. of Boston.

Finally, we wish to express our sincere appreciation to those listed below for their helpfulness to us in our search for material and for suggesting items to be included:

Copley Amory, A. H. Anderson, Arthur B. Appleton, Mrs. Edward S. Baker, W. A. Barron, the late Elmer H. Bartlett, Florence L. Batson,

Charles S. Bird, Jr., Dr. Harold Bowditch, Mrs. Ralph Bradley, Morgan B. Brainard, Ellis W. Brewster, Clarence S. Brigham, Edward A. Bullard, Mrs. Ralph E. Bullard, F. Allen Burt, Philip H. Burt, Godfrey L. Cabot, Mrs. Lilian Carlisle, William E. Chamberlain, Miss C. B. Chapman, Miss Dorothy Cilley, Reginald M. Colby, Charles Coles, Clarkson A. Collins, 3rd, Benjamin F. Conner, Charles H. P. Copeland, W. C. Cousins, the Honorable Louis S. Cox, J. Ralph Cross, Edward Cunningham, Gorham Dana, Edward Dane, Richard H. Davis, Willard F. de Lue, Henry B. L. Dimmick, Miss Margaret A. Dodge, Mrs. Alexander M. Earle, Dean H. Eastman, Frederic B. Eastman, Richard Edgerton, Miss Bessie M. Edson, Kimball C. Elkins, Clarence E. Farrar, Mrs. John A. Figmic, A. Waldo French, Harold W. Gay, Mrs. Herbert F. Georges, Elliott V. Grabill, Mrs. Frank B. Granger, Miss J. L. Harer, Joseph D. Harrington, D. W. Hayward, Ralph N. Hill, Jr., Miss Ruth H. Hill, W. L. Howard, Elmer Munson Hunt, Mrs. Grace Goulder Izant, J. Amory Jeffries, Robert G. Jennings, Walter E. Johnson, James R. Joy, Mrs. Howard W. Kent, Ralph Revere Kent, Emil A. Kessler, James Lawrence, Clifford Lewis, Jr., Mr. and Mrs. Bertram K. Little, Mrs. Harold G. Look, Julian C. Loring, George T. Luby, Acheson E. Lucey, Mrs. Henry Lyman, A. Laurence MacKenzie, Miss Marian MacLeod, W. R. McNeil, Mrs. Amelia E. MacSwiggan, J. Harold Marriott, Mrs. Robert M. May, L. Douglas Meredith, George L. Moore, Mrs. Mary Turner Noyes, Earle W. Newton, William N. Oedel, Robertson Page, Dr. Arthur W. Peach, Robert P. Peckett, Miss Amy Lyman Phillips, James Duncan Phillips, Mrs. Margaret Ann Poole, Harry H. Randall, Mrs. Henry C. Rathbun, Miss Edna L. Ricker, Stephen T. Riley, Rachael Robinson, John R. Russell, E. L. Sanderson, Mrs. Henry Hallam Saunderson, F. A. Schlesinger, Everett W. Smith, Ursula Smith, Frank O. Spinney, Earl W. Stamm, Ernest H. Stevens, Col. Thomas F. Sullivan, Jason A. Swadkins, L. G. Tasker, Mrs. Harold Taylor, Alan S. Towle, Harry E. Trask, Heaton I. Treadway, Richard F. Treadway, Mrs. C. M. Underhill, Diggory Venn, Charles Edward Verner, Samuel Wakeman, Mrs. J. Watson Webb, Mrs. George B. Wells, Mrs. Barbara Winbourne, Edwin B. Worthen and William H. Young.

In the collection of the
STATE STREET TRUST COMPANY
at its Main Office

From an old Tavern built by Jesse Healy in 1805 in South Charlestown, New Hampshire, not far from Hillsboro. This sign shows the Masonic emblem — the square and compass.

Photograph by G. M. Cushing, Jr.

IT *has been our custom to issue from time to time publications designed to prove enjoyable and of historical value to our friends. We trust that this thirty-eighth brochure will succeed in fulfilling this desire.*

We also hope that the impression received will be so favorable that the reader will feel that our publications typify the institution which issues them and that the high standard maintained in their form and material is characteristic of the banking and trust service we render. Opportunities to demonstrate that fact are always welcome.

We shall be very happy if the pleasure derived from our brochures induces our friends to think favorably of the State Street Trust Company when the occasion arises for opening a new bank account, using our comprehensive foreign banking service, financing the purchase of an automobile or household appliances, or renting a safe deposit box at any of our four offices. We also have storage facilities for silverware and other bulky valuables at our Massachusetts Avenue office.

It may be that some of our readers are not aware of the fact that our Trust Department is qualified by experience to serve effectively as Agent in the handling of investments, as Trustee of Living Trusts, Pension and Profit Sharing Plans, Life Insurance Trusts, as Executor and Trustee under wills and in any other recognized trust capacity.

It will be a pleasure to us to furnish to those interested detailed information in regard to any of the various services which we render.

ALLAN FORBES,
Chairman of the Board
State Street Trust Company

Boston, 1954

"Boston has opened and kept open more turnpikes that lead straight to free thought and free speech and free deeds than any other city of live or dead men."

OLIVER WENDELL HOLMES

Taverns and Stagecoaches

of

New England

VOLUME II

TABLE OF CONTENTS

	PAGE
TRAVEL IN THE EARLY DAYS	1
TAVERNS AND THEIR LANDLORDS	8
SOME TAVERNS OF OLD BOSTON	13
BUNCH OF GRAPES TAVERN, BOSTON	18
GREEN DRAGON TAVERN, BOSTON	25
STAVERS STARTS BOSTON'S FIRST STAGECOACH LINE	28
WHITE MOUNTAIN COACHING PARADES	30
EAGLE TAVERN, EAST POULTNEY, VERMONT	42
SHELBURNE, VERMONT MUSEUM AND ITS STAGECOACH INN	49
RED LION INN, STOCKBRIDGE, MASS.	52
EAGLE HOUSE, HAVERHILL, MASS.	57
HORSE MARINE NEWS	59
PUBLICK HOUSE, STURBRIDGE, MASS.	63
GROTON INN	65
BUCKMAN TAVERN, LEXINGTON, MASS.	69
MUNROE TAVERN, LEXINGTON, MASS.	72
PISTOL ORNAMENTATION OF STAGECOACH DAYS	78
PUNCH BOWL TAVERN, BROOKLINE	81
THE "OLD ORDINARY," HINGHAM, MASS.	85
THE TREE OF KNOWLEDGE, DUXBURY, MASS.	90
DOTY TAVERN, PONKAPOAG, CANTON, MASS.	94
THE MORSE AND OTHER EARLY TAVERNS OF WALPOLE, MASS.	97
ISRAEL HATCH, STAGECOACH AND TAVERN MOGUL	101
CHERRY TAVERN, PONKAPOAG, CANTON, MASS.	106
RARE TAVERN SIGNBOARDS	108
SOME CONNECTICUT TAVERN STORIES	111
OTHER NEW ENGLAND SIGNBOARDS	112
THE COMING OF THE IRON HORSE	118

The Bettmann Archive

From a drawing by T. de Thulstrup

A Relay on the Old Boston Post Road

Taverns and *Stagecoaches*

of

New England

TRAVEL IN THE EARLY DAYS

IT WAS MANY YEARS after the landing of the Pilgrims at Plymouth before land travel by wagon and coach began to develop. The first settlers found a complete wilderness, of course, and located their homes along the rivers and bays close to water transportation. Much of the early travel was by water, and those going inland went by foot or horseback. In New England the winter pedestrian used snowshoes and carried a pole having a large wooden disk at its bottom for extra support — a crude type of the modern ski pole. Mail service by post riders began in 1693. The mail man traveled by horse and, besides the mail, carried articles for people along his route. He did all sorts of errands: distributed the news when there were no newspapers; paid and collected bills; encouraged the wayside inns; protected such as needed a responsible guide in their travels and served the people all around, being known and trusted and liked. The Government apparently did not mind as long as it did not interfere with the carrying of the mail. The roads were little more than widened bridle paths, making travel slow, uncertain and uncomfortable. Conditions were much improved by the coming of the privately-owned turnpikes. It was then that stage-coach lines developed rapidly and many freight-hauling enter-prises were established. Taverns were built to accommodate highway travelers, and many of them remained as historic land-marks long after the travel they served had ceased. It is these stagecoach lines and taverns which we have endeavored to tell about in an interesting way in this volume. The early stage-coaches were little more than covered wagons with three benches without backs set one behind the other with the driver's seat outside. The only entrance was at the front of the wagon, so late comers seeking rear seats were forced to climb over those in front. Women were generally given the rear seats because of the support for their backs afforded by the rear of the wagon. Since they were almost always the last to arrive, they afforded the gentlemen much amusement in their efforts to reach their seats. At one period the vehicles had long bodies set on very low springs, with seats for five passengers. There was no door, so passengers entered at the front on their hands and knees and crawled to their seats. The coach with the egg-shaped body was introduced in 1818 and was a great improvement but in 1827 coach travel was revolutionized by the introduction of the Concord coach which met with immediate favor as it was so much more com-fortable than its predecessors. This stagecoach, which was such an important factor in the development of transportation, reached its heyday during the first thirty years of the 19th Century. Highway travel became so active that Badger & Porter's STAGE REGISTER (a form of time-table) published from 1825 until 1834, was a very necessary source of information as to the various stage lines and their schedules. As they announced in presenting the second volume of their publication, the pub-lishers had this to say: "The facilities for internal communication and the conveyances of traveling have increased within a few years, in such an astonishing degree, that a Register of the whole is not only a desideratum but almost *indispensable* to the tourist." This REGISTER was published every two months as a supplement to the "American Traveller" published Tuesday and Friday mornings by Willard Badger and Royal L. Porter, 72 Market Street, Boston. Changes in service, or the addition of new stage lines, which took place between the issues of the REGISTER, were reported in the "American Traveller."

All this traffic naturally meant business for the innkeepers.

Coaches usually traveled at the rate of four or five miles an hour with a change of horses every ten miles. This gave passengers the opportunity to refresh themselves at the taverns along the way. It was customary for the stage to arrive at an inn at the hour of noon when a hearty dinner, the chief meal of the day, was ready for the travelers. When it came to overnight lodging, there was no such thing as a private room. All beds were big enough to accommodate at least two persons and frequently there were as many as three beds in a room. The tavern keeper did not consider his house filled until every bed was yielding at least double income. If a guest wanted a bath or a fire in the room, there was an extra charge. The fire was kindled to order in the fireplace, or stove, and the bath was taken in a wooden tub which a porter filled with hot water carried up from the kitchen.

The stagecoach succumbed to the competition of the railroads which in Massachusetts began in 1834 with the operation of the Boston & Worcester Railroad. Naturally enough, the first railroad cars resembled in many ways the stagecoaches which they were soon to replace, just as the first automobiles were called "horseless carriages," because the first experimental cars were similar to the older vehicles, equipped with motors to replace the pulling power of the horses.

In most of the early Massachusetts charters for the operation of turnpike roads it was directed that they should be built in as straight a line as possible, which resulted in going up and down hill regardless of grades. A Massachusetts farmer who tried to promote a more practical method, such as is common today, used as his argument: "I'll say agin, as I've said afore, that the bail of a kettle is just as long standing up as it is laying down."

The Massachusetts custom was to require that on each turnpike tollgate a signboard be posted displaying the rates "fairly and legibly written thereon in large or capital letters." While rates varied, of course, the following schedule is fairly typical:

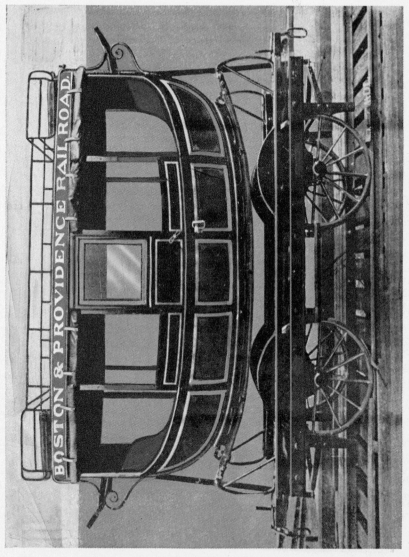

Courtesy Frederic C. Dumaine, Jr., President, New York, New Haven & Hartford Railroad

ORIGINAL BOSTON & PROVIDENCE RAILROAD CAR JUNE 4, 1834

Like most of the early cars used by railroads, it will be noticed that this one is really a stagecoach adapted to the new form of transportation.

Rates of Toll

For every coach, phaeton, chariot or other four-wheeled
carriage drawn by two horses.................... 25 cents

And if drawn by more than two horses, for each additional horse............................... 4 cents

For every curricle.............................. 17 cents

For every cart, wagon, sled or sleigh drawn by two oxen
or horses.................................... 10 cents

And if drawn by more than two, for each horse or ox in
addition..................................... 3 cents

For every chaise, chair, or other carriage drawn by one
horse....................................... 10 cents

For every sled or sleigh drawn by one horse......... 6 cents

For every man and horse........................ 4 cents

For all oxen, horses, mules, and neat cattle led or driven
besides those in teams and carriages, each......... 1 cent

For all sheep and swine by the dozen.............. 3 cents

Toll gates were generally erected at intervals of about ten
miles. For local reasons a turnpike company was allowed to
establish two gates within the limits of one, collecting one half
the toll rate at each. Such gates were known as "half gates."
Certain persons were exempt from paying toll, such as: "any
person who shall be passing with his horse or carriage to or from
public worship, or with his horse or team to or from any mill,
or with his horse, team, or cattle to or from his ordinary labor
on his farm, or on the common or ordinary business of family
concerns within the same towns; or any person passing on
military duty." If the toll gatherer failed to be at his post, the
gate had to be left open and everybody passed through free of
charge. Also, if a turnpike was ruled by the Court of Common
Pleas to be in bad condition, repairs were ordered to be made,
the gate to be open meanwhile for the free passage of all.

During the winter, wheels on the stagecoaches were sometimes replaced by runners and through the courtesy of J. Ralph

Cross, a former member of the staff of the State Street Trust Company, and Ernest H. Stevens, both of the Pembroke (Mass.) Historical Society, we are able to include here a rare picture of a coach so equipped which ran on the old Marshfield-Hanover line.

In these old stagecoach days there was a law prohibiting travel on Sunday except from necessity or charity — a law which was not repealed until 1887. One of the most amusing stories we ran across pertaining to this statute was attributed to Andover. Disturbed by violations of the law, the citizens of that town determined to see that it was enforced. One of the deacons of the church was appointed to see that the officers performed their duties and stationed himself with them at a toll gate just outside the town. A gentleman traveling in a carriage was stopped and told that he could go no farther. He very courteously congratulated the guardians on their desire to enforce the law which was familiar to him but asked that he be permitted to pass as his mother was lying dead in Boston. The deacon and the officers conferred on this and decided that the traveler was within his rights and allowed him to continue on his journey. When he had reached a safe distance, he called back, "Don't forget to tell the good people of Andover that you permitted me to pass because my mother is lying dead in Boston. You may add, also, if you please, that she has been lying dead there for some twenty years."

One interesting, and as far as we have discovered, unique sidelight on early travel was brought to our attention by our Director, Edward Cunningham. Through his thoughtful interest, we were privileged to see a letter written in September of 1792 by an ancestor of his friend Clifford Lewis, Jr., of Philadelphia. This described a visit to Boston which was during an epidemic of smallpox, when all who left the town had to be fumigated. To quote from the letter, written by David Lewis: "Luckily for us on entering the Town last Evening our Stage broke down, whereby we were enabled to enjoy a full Prospect of the smoking Business. A sort of Sentry Box & a strong Guard is fixed on each Side of the Road where every Person going out of Town must bring too & stand a few Minutes fastened up in one of these Boxes, and in which they have a constant Fire & keep applying their infernal Combustible — I had some hearty laughs at the Smoaked, for which the Smoakers have threatened me pretty hard on going out — but I mean to give them Gentry the Slip & pass by the other smoke House where by Compliance I hope to be treated with Levity." He also wrote that when he left Boston that evening for Portsmouth he intended to take all of his silk stockings into the Smoke House with him in order to have them bleached!

It is difficult for the current generation to realize that at the end of the 19th Century, nearly 300 years after the first settlement at Plymouth, our nation's roads were chiefly plain earth surfaces which were almost impassable in wet weather, so our tremendous highway systems of today are really a fairly modern development. The automobile, of course, has been the greatest reason for the rapid improvement of our present millions of miles of highways.

TAVERNS
and
THEIR LANDLORDS

THE AGREEABLE and the disagreeable landlord are well described by Edward Field in his *The Colonial Tavern*. He quotes a writer as saying:

> . . . some landlords were so full of sunshine that it was June all the year round; others had minds so frost-bitten that there was no hope for you except in the January thaw. Here was one so anxious to oblige that he would spring to throw a lassoo around the moon if you wished it, and then another so cross that putting a question to him was like squeezing a lemon.

As a rule, adds Field, the landlord of the tavern was a man whose company was sought for its cheer and comfort.

The innkeeper's duties were varied and strenuous, according to this same authority:

> He led the singing in the meeting house on Sunday; ran the ferry if his tavern was situated beside a stream; acted as schoolmaster for the children of those who frequented his house; served his fellow men in the legislature, town council, selectman, and other minor offices; ruled with solemn dignity over the local courts; headed the Train Band on training or squadron days; kept order in the meeting house on Sundays . . .

A traveler in this country thought that innkeepers would not "put themselves into a bustle on your account;" but with "good language," he added, "they are very civil and will accommodate you as well as they can."

An article in the Fitchburg Historical Society, written by Frederick A. Currier, recalls these words of a traveler: "The eating was the cream of the earth. I dined last week at Delmonico's and my dinner was nothing to the cutlets, the ham and eggs, and johnny-cakes of the old Tavern days."

The well publicized Boston widow, Sarah Knight, had

Connecticut line, and in exchange she turned over to Connecticut an equivalent area of 40,000 acres—thus accounting for the unusual name given above. After Connecticut had come into possession of this great timber tract of pine, she was at a loss as to what to do with it. It was too far away to be available in the wooden nutmeg trade, therefore the lands were auctioned off at a public sale and the proceeds given to Yale College. Thus, the first extensive real estate transaction in those parts was sort of a benefit performance. Two years after this transaction took place William Brattle, William Dummer and others who had bought the property sight unseen, at the price of a farthing an acre, met at the duly-proclaimed meeting at the *Green Dragon* to form an organization for the disposition and development of their property. It was, presumably, at this meeting that Mr. Brattle came into possession of the area located in the immediate vicinity of the attractive, bustling town which in its name now preserves the memory of this Massachusetts loyalist, one of the original patentees.

It was not until around 1753 that settlement began in Brattleboro but it prospered and became incorporated ten years later.

From a sketch by Emil A. Kessler, Staff Artist of the "Boston Sunday Post"

STAVERS STARTS BOSTON'S FIRST STAGECOACH LINE

JONATHAN WARDWELL set up a hackney coach stand in 1712 at his *Orange Tree Tavern* at the head of Hanover Street, and on May 13 of 1718 advertised a coach leaving for Rhode Island. However, the first public stagecoach line, operating on a regular schedule, seems to have been the one established by Bartholomew Stavers, with headquarters at the *Sign of the Lighthouse* in the North End of Boston, not far from Old North Church. The route was between Boston and Portsmouth, N. H. and the year was 1761. The reason given was "for the encouragement of trade between these two places." The first vehicle used was what Stavers described as "a large stage chair" drawn by two horses and guaranteed to seat four passengers. In less than six weeks, such was the success of the venture, conveyances to accommodate five people were put into use. In May of 1763 the "Portsmouth Flying Stagecoach" was launched, carrying six passengers inside.

For the purpose of saving the cost and trouble of ferrying, there being no bridges at that time, the stages and horses were kept at Charlestown from which place they started every Friday morning. The return from Portsmouth, after the new vehicles were put in operation, was every Tuesday morning. On the trip from Portsmouth to Boston, a stop was made at Ipswich for lodging overnight. In the morning the stage resumed its journey to Boston, going around by way of Medford and across Charlestown Neck to the ferry where it arrived the second night after leaving Portsmouth, if all went well. This trip would take about two hours by automobile today; a little over an hour by railroad and less than an hour by plane.

The enterprising Stavers put out notices to the effect that

as this was a convenient and genteel way of traveling and greatly cheaper (13s6d) than hiring horses or carriages, he hoped the ladies and gentlemen would encourage the same. The stage-coaches did much to liven up the countryside through which they passed and were a welcome sight to farmers and to those in isolated hamlets who saw little of the outside world.

The great increase in travel and business following the peace of 1763 which abolished our French frontier and threw the "Eastward" open to American settlers, encouraged Stavers to employ a coach-and-four which he boasted was always on time and never lost a passenger or package. When needs demanded, he put six horses to his coach, and so regular was his service that it attracted what the law required should be sent by mail. The postal authorities remonstrated and threatened, but the public demanded that Stavers should carry its letters, therefore the case was settled by establishing an additional mail which was carried by the Stavers coaches. This is said to be the first mailcoach in the history of the British Empire.

The Stavers coaches appear to have been built by Adino Paddock of Boston. He and Stavers were loyalists and when the Revolution came both went to England to live. It was natural that they should talk a lot about the American stage-coach and mailcoach service, with the result that John Palmer brought the matter to the personal notice of William Pitt, second son of the Earl of Chatham, friend of America, who authorized Palmer to establish similar mail service in England. Thus, the Massachusetts idea was adopted by that nation in 1784.

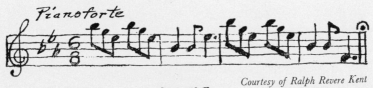

Courtesy of Ralph Revere Kent

HOME.

OLD TRUMPET CALL OF STAGECOACH DRIVERS IN ENGLAND

WHITE MOUNTAIN
COACHING PARADES

THESE COACHING PARADES from 1887 to 1897 were gay and attractive, and brought visitors from all directions. Some of the really old stagecoaches that had done service were polished up and reinforced for these festive occasions, while other vehicles of a more modern brand were added to the scene. The old stagecoaches created, of course, special interest. A feature of the earliest event was the appearance of George Lane who, as the newspaper *Among the Clouds* reported, "cracked the same whip which he carried when he drove the first coach to the top of Mount Washington a quarter of a century previously." The Crawford House sent a stagecoach that had been used for a number of years around Crawford Notch and nearby resorts. Other well known stages represented the Fabyan and Mount Pleasant Houses.

Amy Lyman Phillips wrote for the *White Mountain Echo* for a few years and recently contributed stories in the *Littleton Courier*. In a letter to us last summer she recalls that Peckett's on Sugar Hill had the most beautiful of all coaches in their

Courtesy of New Hampshire Profiles

UNUSUAL PICTURE OF A STAGECOACH ON TOP OF MT. WASHINGTON, NEW HAMPSHIRE

Courtesy of Miss Amy Lyman Phillips

CRAWFORD HOUSE STAGECOACH

Used in some of the White Mountain parades and elsewhere, it was one of the really old stages. This picture was taken about the year 1909. The large (lighter colored) mountain in the background is Mt. Webster, named for Daniel Webster. The mountain that rises at the right, behind the railway station, is Mt. Willard. The veteran driver, George Howland, was renowned in his day for guiding a team of six among the hills.

collection of historic vehicles. Not long ago a fire destroyed them, but fortunately she had a picture which she loaned us to reproduce in this chapter.

In the first parade, held in 1887, the Maplewood Cottage showed a "bevy of beauties that quickly put the hearts of the gilded youth into a fluttering condition." Not to be outdone, the Strawberry Hill House exhibited a coach whose top was covered by "Champion beauties," and the "Witchery of feminine loveliness." One hotel had the "prettiest load of fair sex," while another contained "beauties with bewitching smiles." The seats on one vehicle were filled with "nymphs." Fabyan's brought forth the complimentary remark that "every lady on the coach was a prize in herself."

Among the Clouds mentioned particularly the occupants of

AT THE WHITE MOUNTAINS

From an old print owned by William N. Oedel, Vice-President, State Street Trust Company

At the White Mountains

Courtesy of Robert P. Peckett and Miss Amy Lyman Phillips

PECKETT COACH AT THE MAPLEWOOD HOTEL

the Bellevue coach, stating that "in their gorgeousness they placed Joseph's coat of many colors far into the shade," and that the onlookers were "struck dumb with amazement."

The *Echo* declared that "even Newport would have received an awakening impulse from the gay pageant which brightened Bethlehem Street" in this inaugural parade of 1887, a visitor from New York remarking that it was "the biggest thing that ever occurred in the White Mountains." After this parade a Mrs. Morrison of Boston appeared on the balcony of the Maplewood Hotel as the Goddess of Liberty.

In the 1888 parade the Hotel Lookoff coach bore a quotation from Virgil "Sic itur ad astra," meaning "Thus one goes to the stars." Prizes were presented at the close of each parade and the Chairman of the 1888 event made this amusing remark: "If you had sent these pretty ladies down south thirty years ago, you would have saved a great deal of ammunition (applause) for they would have converted every man of that section from

Courtesy of F. Allen Burt and Miss Edna L. Ricker

A Well Decorated White Mountain Stagecoach Ready for One of the Parades

The building in the picture is the McMillan House. Teams composed of white horses were especially attractive. Many of the horses were used in lumber camps during the winters.

a supporter of the doctrine of secession to a warm advocate of an indissoluble Union."

In the 1889 event the Sinclair coach was referred to in *Among the Clouds* as "fit for Queens," adding that when it passed the judges' stand "the spectators nearly exhausted their vocabulary of adjectives of laudation."

This same year the Crawfords sang an amusing rhyme which seemed to make a decided hit. The first verse read:

> A gallant young freshman was riding
> On the top of a big tally-ho
> With a sweet girl on either side smiling
> And the chaperon nailed in below.

A "Swan" coach from Highland House took the beauty prize in 1889, and *Among the Clouds* stated that the Maplewood entry was amusing to the "button-bursting degree." The *White Mountain Echo* reported that this parade was a great success and that the news of this event spread throughout a good part of the country. It was as important, added this newssheet, as "an International Yacht Race, the Derby and the University Boat Races of England, the Sengerfests of Germany, the Venetian Fête of Geneva, the Rose Festival of Nice, or the Ice Carnival of Canada, or the Mardi Gras festivities of New Orleans."

Each vehicle was decorated by the hotel visitors and they made pretty sights. The papers were flattering, one, in describing a parade, declaring that "visions of lovely women, magnificent horses, superb trappings and beautifully decorated coaches floated by," each one with its favorite yell or song.

The eyes of the many spectators were attracted particularly to the tops of the vehicles, which were filled chiefly by the fair sex representing the many hotels and localities. A careful study of these events found in *Among the Clouds* and the *White Mountain Echo*, in the Boston Public Library, brought forth detailed descriptions and it would seem that each account vied with the other in praising the effect produced by the women.

Pagodas, Turkish, Japanese and Chinese costumes, Roman

Courtesy F. Allen Burt and Miss Edna L. Ricker

BEAUTIFULLY DECORATED KEARSARGE HOUSE COACH IN THE PARADE OF 1895

Charioteers and Abenakis Indians from Canada were occasionally in evidence. Of course Martha and George Washington appeared, and Columbus and Hiawatha drove by on different coaches. Bicycles, ridden by both sexes, also took part in the later events.

Neptune's Chariot and Cleopatra's Barge from Twin Mountain House were shown in the 1890 parade. "Diana's Baths" took the whole of the top of one coach, described by the *White Mountain Echo*, "with their limpid contents in which the Goddess of the Chase may have played the part of a mermaid, for aught we know."

In the 1892 parade the famous Keeley Institute of North Conway (known better to some people than to others) was represented. One old coach in this parade came from a distance of sixty-five miles, receiving an ovation.

The judging was very difficult and one official who was unable to procure a lunch said that a "hungry jury always finds for the wrong side, therefore I ask your indulgence."

In this same year the top of one coach was filled with Japanese gowned girls, being declared "a freight of fair yum-yums." Two years later, in order to out-do their rivals in gaudy styles the girls wore thin costumes and as the day was on the cool side they looked rather shivery. The *Echo* float counteracted with this banner:

> Hurrah for the girls,
> Hurrah for the white;
> We're not frozen,
> We're all right.

A few of the coaches and tally-hos were fitted up to represent many scenes and characters, not going as far back, however, as Adam and Eve! One float showed the effect of the Twentieth Century Girl on the summer resorts, but no details were announced by the papers. The Maine Central Railroad, rather singularly, showed a facsimile of one of the steamers that used to ply between Rockland and Bar Harbor, probably the

J. T. Morse, whose fame was well known for its many trips on the water and also sometimes beneath the water.

The Bethlehem coach, in 1896, caused much laughter by appearing with sixteen women and one forlorn looking man. Another vehicle from Bellevue House exhibited a placard reading:

> Well, well, well!
> Aren't we sweet,
> We're from the Bellevue
> On Bethlehem Street.

Six well matched bays drew a vehicle from the Poland Spring House containing "fourteen visions of loveliness personified" and following this entry came a coach with college men who caused much laughter by singing this *un*rhyme:

> Do you see these girls before us?
> Well they perfectly adore us,
> And, ye terrors! how they bore us!
> For they're nearly two to one.
> They certainly are pretty,
> But isn't it a pity,
> That out of some great city,
> They didn't bring just one man apiece.

On the Mount Pleasant coach, drawn by six "prancing" blacks were girls who "depicted America's highest society life."

New Hampshire must have been searched far and wide to collect the hundreds of horses that made up the four-in-hands and the six-in-hands seen in the pictures reproduced here; in one case eight steeds, all white, drew the Sinclair House coach. The color scheme of the horses was adhered to in most cases, many matched bays, chestnuts and blacks predominating. There were one or more teams of greys and whites and one would like to know where these were found for each of the eight annual parades that were held during these years, with only two omissions, 1891 and 1893. We have been told that many of the horses worked in the New Hampshire logging camps during the winter. F. Allen Burt, who has helped us a great deal, recalls that Col. Joseph M. Thompson, at one time owner of the first

Glen House in Pinkham Notch, had a driver so efficient with his team of eight perfectly matched whites that he could, from a gallop, time his Concord coach to pull up at the Grand Trunk Station at Gorham exactly upon the arrival of the train.

These coaching events brought many persons to the White Mountains, spoken of as the "Switzerland of America" on Carrigain's 1816 Map of New Hampshire. Charlotte Cushman was mentioned as very fond of "stage coach riding," and Daniel Webster often visited there, riding in a White Mountain stagecoach, the driver bragging, according to Fabyan's correspondent of the *Boston Herald*, that he used to bring Webster his cider and doughnuts. Governor Eben S. Draper often visited the Granite Hills, as they have been termed, and to quote Miss Phillips again, most of Ward McAllister's "pets" visited there during a season. The mountains also attracted P. T. Barnum, who showed his pleasure in having just procured what he termed a "corkscrew" man, adding to his friends that he was prepared to give $20,000 for a sea serpent. He pronounced the view from the summit of Mount Washington to be "the second greatest show on earth." A William L. Webster of Boston often served as Chief Marshal of the Coaching Parades.

Among the Clouds was issued twice daily during the summer on the summit of Mount Washington (6293 feet above the sea) from 1877 to 1907. It was the only newspaper ever printed on the top of any mountain in the world, and was published by Henry M. Burt of Springfield, Massachusetts, until his death in 1897. His son, Frank H. Burt of Newton, Massachusetts, continued the publication of this unique newssheet until the Great Fire of June 1908 destroyed the printing office along with all the other buildings on the summit with the exception of the old stone Tiptop House. The latter's son, F. Allen Burt of Brookline, Massachusetts, discovered among his collection of White Mountain material some pictures, here reproduced, and accounts of many interesting incidents. He is completing a History of Mount Washington, featuring the story of *Among the*

Clouds; therefore we have left that part to him, and confined ourselves to the parades "below the clouds."

The "Coaching Parade" editions of *Among the Clouds* were sped down the cog railway early in the morning after the parades by a group of expert slide-board riders. A wagon with a team of fast horses awaited their arrival at the Base Station in order to catch the early trains at Fabyan's in time to score a "scoop" on all city newspapers. Special emphasis was given these detailed accounts of the parades at Bethlehem and North Conway. The names of many visitors to the mountains were noted in these two daily editions, which also printed the news of the different resorts. The author's eye caught the attraction of a big black bear that was being exhibited one season in various towns for a number of days. A feature another summer was a female barber at Fabyan's who seemed to be quite popular.

The other newspaper, *The White Mountain Echo,* showing on the cover a boy blowing a horn, with a mountain in the distance, was printed once a week at Bethlehem beginning in the year 1887, by an Englishman named Addey. For a time it was leased and conducted by Miss Amy Lyman Phillips, who has assisted us with excerpts and photographs. Miss Phillips has vivid memories of the splendor of these parades and fairly recently described these events in the *Littleton Courier* in various articles which have been both interesting and helpful to this chapter. Both newspapers appeared only during the summer months. The well known Sanford's Ginger contributed a good many advertisements and was called "a friend in need" . . . "cures everything." There were continual advertisements also of the Hotel Vendome "Boston's new and most superb hotel." The hills were spoken of as the best means to "assassinate hay fever."

The Great White Hills of New Hampshire by the late Ernest Poole sums up these activities so attractively that we have thought it well to get permission to add this paragraph:

From a photograph by   *Courtesy of F. Allen Burt*
The Hall Studio, Littleton, N. H.

A WHITE MOUNTAIN COACHING PARADE AT BETHLEHEM, NEW HAMPSHIRE

This is one of the few pictures showing a line of coaches.

All through the Eighties and Nineties, the Coach Parade at Bethlehem was the big show event of the year. It came in the late summer; and some forty coaches, together with tallyhos and dogcarts behind tandems, took part. From scores of summer hotels they came with gay parties to spend the day. To the music of coach horns and a band, the parade pranced down the main street to the Maplewood Hotel and back, while the judges from their stand watched not only the driving and teams but the decorations on each coach or tallyho. Each hotel had its own color; and with flowers and paper ribbons streaming in the breeze and lady passengers arrayed in bonnets and picture hats, fluffy gowns and parasols, all in shades of the chosen color, each strained to make its coach the very loveliest in the show. Old ladies still sigh as they look back to the bustles and wasp waists, the bonnets, hats and parasols, jingling harness, high-stepping teams and melodious coach horns of that day.

An annual parade of the old time stages takes place at Deadwood, South Dakota, each year and Donald H. McLaughlin, President of the Homestake Mining Company, sent the account of last August's interesting event, showing several Concord stages that were used on the Deadwood-Cheyenne line.

All the coaches used in both the New Hampshire and Deadwood parades were manufactured by the Abbot-Downing Company of Concord, New Hampshire, described in our 1953 brochure.

EAGLE TAVERN
East Poultney, Vermont

From a charcoal drawing by the late Roy F. Heinrich

A VERMONT TOAST OF REVOLUTIONARY DAYS FIRST GIVEN
AT EAGLE TAVERN, EAST POULTNEY, VERMONT

"To the enemies of our country! May they have cobweb breeches,
a porcupine saddle, a hard trotting horse and an eternal journey!"

THE ABOVE illustration and caption are used through the
courtesy of The National Life Insurance Company of Montpelier,
Vermont, and seem to be an appropriate introduction to our
story of this old Vermont tavern.

It may be recalled by some of our readers that we mentioned

this famous toast in last year's brochure. Since then we have had much pleasant correspondence with Walter E. Johnson, the present proprietor of *Eagle Tavern*, where the toast is said to have been given originally by Captain William Watson.

The facts leading to the purchase of the old tavern by Mr. and Mrs. Johnson make quite a story which was very well told in the 1953 Summer Issue of "Vermont Life," that excellent, beautifully illustrated magazine published quarterly by the Vermont Development Commission.

In one of his letters, Mr. Johnson termed his story a report on their "Tavern-daze." One paragraph, quoted below, should make pleasant reading, especially to New Englanders, native or adopted.

" 'Go West, Young Man' may or may not still be good advice — if it ever was. I followed it nearly forty years ago and it is no exaggeration when I say that for thirty-five years there was never a minute when I was not conscious of the lack of that something which New England alone, of all sections of the country, has which gives life its *fullest* meaning. The longer I am back here, the more I begrudge the time that I was away — and the more anxious I am to let others know how strongly I feel about it."

After spending the summer of 1950 on the shore of St. Albans Bay, the Johnsons decided to rent a small furnished apartment and see how it would be to live through a Vermont winter, which might be rather rugged. An enterprising real estate man showed them the vacant *Eagle Tavern* which was furnished but was for sale — not for rent. The handsome structure, reminiscent of southern colonial buildings, seemed huge but was available immediately, and they were told that the entire second floor could be closed off easily when not needed. Although, obviously, it was not at all what they had in mind, they decided it would do no harm to look over this ancient building of Colonial times. Once inside they discovered many attractive features, but when they climbed on some furniture and, peering at the attic from the trap door, saw the huge 9 x 12 hardwood beams, all notched together and fastened with wooden pegs, solid as the day they were first raised, they

Courtesy Walter E. Johnson, present proprietor of this ancient hostelry

EAGLE TAVERN, EAST POULTNEY, VERMONT
WHICH DATES BACK TO COLONIAL DAYS

were convinced that life could not be complete without possessing this gem of early American architecture. Having made up their minds to purchase the historic hostelry, they also decided that the only logical thing to do was to reopen its rooms to the traveling public, thus fulfilling the destiny from which it had been temporarily diverted.

Vermont history, and particularly the history of *Eagle Tavern*, became one of the immediate studies of the Johnson family. They discovered that the Tavern had been one of the important focal points of our Revolutionary struggles. Here Ethan Allen had dared, with Remember Baker and Robert Cochran, to pen the bold "Poster of Defiance" in 1772 against the King's henchmen in Albany. Three years later men had gathered there on their venturesome way to capture Fort Ticonderoga. Also, the victorious Green Mountain Boys probably tarried for refreshments there as they sledged the heavy cannon they had captured through the snow to Dorchester Heights to give vital aid to General Washington in forcing the evacuation of Boston. One of Ethan Allen's favorite quotations, "The Gods of the Hills are not the Gods of the Valleys," now embellishes the frieze in the entrance hall of the Tavern. In Colonial times when the stagecoaches arrived at East Poultney the passengers separated according to their politics — those with thoughts of revolution in their minds putting up at *Eagle Tavern*, while the Tories lodged at a nearby inn known as the *Rising Sun Tavern*. Later *Eagle Tavern* became an overnight stop on the stage run from Lansingburg, N. Y., to Burlington. The Tory tavern is now used as the village Post Office.

In the late eighteen-twenties Horace Greeley had lived here when Harlow and Sarah Hosford were the owners, and when he left the town to go west in 1830 he wore a suit made for him by "Aunt Sally" Hosford. It was across the green from the Tavern that he gave his first political speech in the "Academy" which was built in 1791 and is now being restored as a museum. In his autobiography, Greeley reveals the depth of his feeling about East Poultney in these words: "I have never since known a community so generally moral, intelligent, industrious, and friendly — never one where so much good was known and so little evil said of neighbor by neighbor," and over a century later the Johnsons re-echo identical sentiments. Two of the many items of historic and sentimental interest to be seen at the Tavern are a type case at which Greeley learned to set type and a rare copy of the *Northern Spectator* on which he worked — gifts of thoughtful friends who felt the Tavern where he lived the appropriate place for them to be preserved and to be seen by those interested. One of the guests of the Tavern in 1953, by the way, was Horace Greeley Fowler, a descendant of the illustrious Horace. Portraits of Harlow and Sarah Hosford adorn the walls of the Tavern, gifts from an elderly lady of the town. Hanging in the library is the deed of 1825 by which the Hosfords acquired title to the property, a fixture attached to the building in accordance with the stipulation of intervening owners who, correctly and with generous foresight, wanted it always to remain affixed to the property.

In 1838 Hosford, according to an item in the *Rutland Herald* of March 20th of that year, "banished all intoxicating liquors from his bar and established a temperance House of entertainment." A goodly number of citizens friendly to the cause of temperance assembled at the Tavern on the 13th of March to partake of a public dinner. One of the resolutions passed at the dinner was: "That in consideration of the sacrifice made by Mr. Hosford in discontinuing the sale of intoxicating liquors at his public house, we will, on this *special occasion* pay him double price for our entertainment." Before the resolution could be put to a vote Mr. Hosford stated that he declined any extra compensation as he did not establish a Temperance House to make money out of it, but out of respect to the Temperance Cause. The meeting however "made earnest of the resolution," which we take it means they paid double.

The vaulted "Assembly Room" of the Tavern, as was so frequently the case, was used as a lodge room by Masonic Groups from 1791 to 1817. Cotillions and assemblies, too, were held there. For a period of forty years the Tavern was owned by a man named Buckingham so, inevitably, it became known locally as "Buckingham Palace."

Let us go back now to that Captain William Watson whose name will always be connected with the toast quoted at the head of this chapter. Born in Hartford, Connecticut, in 1748, he became an ardent patriot while working as a mechanic in Hampshire County, Massachusetts, and took upon himself the organization of a company of minutemen. On the morning of April 20, 1775, "exchanging his hammer for the musket" he led his group toward Boston to which Earl Percy's army had retreated under fire following the April 19th affray. By 1779, Watson had become a Captain of Infantry and at the close of the War was brevetted a Major. He was a brave and able officer who gave the best years of his life to the Revolutionary Cause, later coming to disappointment and poverty without complaint. He saw a great deal of action during the War and was greatly admired and loved by his men, who in after years called him "their good and generous old Captain." He apparently was fond of animals, and one of his special pets was a dog he named (in the spirit of the Greek revival) Comus. On the death of his pet he buried him in a wooden box behind *Eagle Tavern*, marking the spot with a stone bearing this inscription:

Comus is dead. Good dog, well bred,

Here he lies — enough is said.

A cherished possession of the Ward family of Poultney is a cane carved by Captain Watson given to the first William Ward, presumably at the banquet at which the Captain made his famous toast. The cane is now owned by William A. Ward, fifth of that name to occupy the family homestead, who, by the way, still operates successfully the ancestral maple sugar "bush." The first William Ward was Justice of the Peace for that area when Vermont was an independent republic (1777–91). He notarized the appraisal of assets in the estate of Heber Allen as rendered in 1784 by his brothers, Ethan and Ira, which is the Number 1 file in the Rutland County Probate Court.

Possibly because his class at Williams College was '14, Mine Host Johnson was particularly impressed by the fact that Vermont was the

Photograph by Miss Dorothy Cilley formerly of the staff of the State Street Trust Co.

REPRODUCTION OF VERMONT'S 14-STAR FLAG OF 1791 ADORNING EAGLE TAVERN, EAST POULTNEY, VT.

fourteenth State to join the Union, and upon initiating research on the subject discovered an old flag in the Bennington Museum which featured a large star surrounded by a circle of thirteen smaller stars. He immediately had a flag made like the original to be hung on the portico of his Tavern as shown in an accompanying illustration. As he says, this "Lone Star" flag of Vermont may never have had any *official* sanction, as Kentucky was admitted to the Union the next year, but for several months in 1791 it would have been valid, and its counterpart might well have been displayed at the old Tavern during that period. At any rate, tradition says that such a flag was flown in Rutland, capital of the Green Mountain Republic, to celebrate Vermont's admission to the Union.

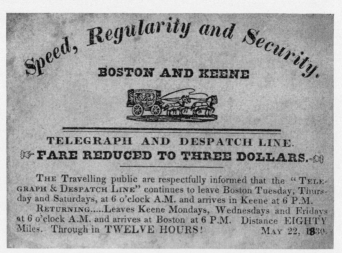

Courtesy T. Therrien, Willimansett, Mass.

SHELBURNE (Vermont) MUSEUM
and its
STAGECOACH INN

IN 1947 MR. AND MRS. J. WATSON WEBB of Shelburne and New York City, who for years had devoted their energies toward preserving treasures of vanishing Americana, constructed the first of a group of buildings characteristic of Vermont and of early New England where their collections could be preserved for the interest of future generations.

It is quite natural that the site selected should be a part of the old town of Shelburne, Vermont, on Lake Champlain, seven miles south of Burlington. The town has been a favorite home of the Webb family ever since the founding of "Shelburne Farms" in 1888 by Dr. W. Seward Webb, father of J. Watson Webb. Dating back to the Revolution, Shelburne is located on Route 7 — the Ethan Allen Highway — which perpetuates the name of the celebrated "father of Vermont." A fourteen-acre plot on the west side of the highway in the center of the village has in six years become the home of the Shelburne Museum.

The first building erected was an immense barn in the shape of a horse-shoe, whose hand-hewn timbers came from eleven old Vermont barns and two grist mills. The structure is now filled with a fascinating array of old time horse-drawn vehicles, including Concord coach Number 23, built by the Abbot-Downing Co. of Concord, N. H. in 1853. In rapid succession came an early 19th century brick schoolhouse from Vergennes, a fine old covered bridge 168 feet long (which leads to the Museum grounds), several early Vermont houses of wood and stone selected for their individual character, a Shaker shed, a brick meeting house, country store and even a lighthouse from the middle of Lake Champlain. These buildings house widely varied collections arranged with such unique good taste that the Museum, even though not yet complete, has already been featured by *Life*, *House and Garden*, *Vogue* and other national magazines.

Mention above of the covered bridge brings to mind an amusing story in the 100th Anniversary booklet issued in 1951 by the National Bank of Derby Line, Vermont. A thrifty Vermonter on reading a sign over a covered bridge which stated "Walk or pay three dollars," got out of his buggy and led his horse, with vehicle attached, through the bridge.

One of the most prominent buildings at Shelburne Museum is the *Stagecoach Inn*. Dating back to 1784 when Vermont was an independent republic, this old tavern has begun a new career as the home of an outstanding collection of folk art — eagles, weathervanes, cigar store Indians, ship figureheads and tavern signs. Originally located in Charlotte, the Inn, like other buildings at the Museum, had an interesting history prior to its removal, plank by plank, to the Museum.

Hezekiah Barnes, a captain in the militia, was a colorful frontiersman who moved his wife and four children into the north country from Lanesboro, Mass. Soon after his arrival in Charlotte he started putting up the stout timbers of his inn. Directly across the road he built a trading post, now Harte's store, and began a flourishing business in butter, cheese and wool. Although he had built his tavern and trading post in a heavily wooded and sparsely settled area, he had, with keen foresight, located it on a road which soon became the main stagecoach line between New York, southern New England and Montreal.

In their search for an authentic old-time tavern, Mr. and Mrs. Webb discovered this almost forgotten *Barnes Tavern* four miles south of Shelburne. Screened from the old stage road by a tangle of trees and shrubs, the building stood empty and forlorn, awaiting eventual decay and destruction. Inspection showed that the hand-hewn beams and walls were as sound as when George Washington was President, and it was decided that it would be a highly appropriate accession to the Shelburne Museum. Elaborate blueprints were prepared and every board and brick identified for use in reassembling the structure.

An indication of the immense amount of detail involved is the fact that roughly 40,000 old bricks were handled in rebuilding the ten fireplaces housing two brick ovens and two ham smoking chambers. Remarkably few replacements in material were necessary. Where they were made, such as in the window casings and chair rails, they were accomplished with the use of old carpenters' planes in the collection of the Museum.

The *Stagecoach Inn*, like the other buildings at the Shelburne Museum, is an enduring reminder not only of the days when New England was young, but of those who are carrying out this reconstruction with such meticulous care. This reconstructed village seems destined to become a popular mecca for those interested in Early Americana.

* * *

THE FOLLOWING old ditty of stagecoach days was sent us by George L. Moore, Public Relations Director of the First National Stores, Inc., and editor of that Company's colorful and interesting magazine "Food Marketing in New England."

> 'Blige the lady,
>   'Blige the lady,
> 'Blige the lady, Sir;
> Says I, "Old chap,
>   She may have my lap
> But I won't stand up for her."
> Then a little fat man,
>   In a little fat voice
> From the opposite corner cried: —
> "If a nice fat lap ain't enough for her,
>   Let the lady ride outside,
> Let the lady ride outside."

RED LION INN
Stockbridge, Mass.

WHILE THE *Red Lion Inn* at Stockbridge has been known by that name since about the year 1900, it came by the name naturally enough because a red lion has been used on its signboard ever since its erection in 1733. During its earlier days it bore the names of Stockbridge House, the Inn, and Plumb's Hotel, always, however, having the Red Lion sign for identification purposes. Until the early 1920's the lion always had a green tail. However, when the

latest sign was made the artist drew a rather skinny lion with the usual green tail. Mr. and Mrs. Plumb's reaction to the first sketch was that they wanted nothing to do with a skinny lion, their lion had to look well-fed and plump in order to typify the high standard of good New England food which had always been served at the Inn. They also decided that a red tail would be preferable to the green one, and that's how it is today. At one time, in addition to the red lion, the crest of the Inn bore on its shield a teapot, plate, Franklin stove, two large keys, a highboy and a clock, symbolic of the collection of antiques on display at the Inn. It also bore the dates 1773 and 1897 — the latter date the year of the completion of the present building which replaced the original structure, destroyed by fire in the autumn of 1896.

Heaton I. Treadway, the present landlord was an infant, about a year old, when the fire occurred. His parents were so busy trying to save their wonderful collection of antiques that they deposited the baby on a trunk in the middle of the street where he had a grand view of the fire which he seemed to enjoy to the full as he kept clapping his hands and laughing at the big bonfire which he took to be arranged for his particular enjoyment.

The tavern was opened for business in 1774 and as its first guests had delegates at a convention to protest against the use of any articles imported from England. Various towns of Berkshire County were represented so the new establishment must have gained a lot of good publicity in the surrounding area by entertaining this group.

Mr. and Mrs. Charles H. Plumb purchased the Inn in 1862. A portrait of the former now hangs in the lobby but tradition says that Mrs. Plumb — "Aunt Mert" as she was called — really deserves the credit for the success of the management. She was loved by all with whom she came in contact and made the Inn one of the most popular of her day. It was her great hobby — antiques — that inspired the collection which is so interesting and valuable today. She had a great sense of humor and one of her favorite stories was about the two collectors of antiques who were at the opera and, in spite of the loud music, were comparing sofas they owned. Suddenly the music stopped and the audience heard one of the *grandes dames* say: "My front feet are beautifully carved with claw and ball." Mrs. Plumb had a standing offer for the old road peddlers who were so numerous years ago — "Fifty cents for any teapot and a dollar for any mirror." As a result of her efforts and inspiration the collection at the Inn, while not the largest, is generally regarded by experts as in a class by itself as far as colonial furniture and crockery are concerned. Mrs. Plumb, herself, obtained most of the authentic old furniture by picking up items in the homes and farms of Berkshire County where she took frequent drives for that purpose.

The late Congressman, Allen T. Treadway, a nephew of Mrs. Plumb, in due course took over the management of the Inn. Before his election to Congress, he had been President of the Massachusetts Senate. On his leaving that office he was presented by his associates with a desk and chair which are now used by his son at the Inn. As a boy, the Congressman remembered hearing the oldest inhabitants describe the tavern sign adorned with the green-tailed lion and also the flurry of activity when the stagecoaches stopped at the Inn to change horses and to allow the passengers to partake of milk punch or hot toddy. Originally the barroom was one of the prominent features of the tavern and very well patronized. Also, as was customary, there was a ball room on the upper floor where people from the surrounding area gathered frequently for the "assemblies" which were so popular in the social life of the time. Additions were made from time to time to the structure so that by 1884 it was of sufficient size to accommodate as many as one hundred guests. When the present building was constructed, it was in a period when it was considered unsanitary to sleep in a room adjoining a toilet. Because of this only two private bath rooms were provided in the whole establishment. (Of course, this situation was changed for the better many years ago.) It was customary then for season guests to bring their own bath tubs and it was nothing out of the ordinary after the arrival of the evening train to have to deliver twenty or twenty-five bath tubs an evening to the rooms, along with trunks and other luggage. The natural sequence was not too much appreciated by the maids of the Inn as they had to take on the onerous duty of carrying hot water to the various rooms which harbored the traveling bath tubs.

The Red Lion, with the green or red tail, during a long life witnessed many varying scenes, from the turbulent and distressful days of 1786–7, when Stockbridge was one of the centers of hostilities during Shays's Rebellion, to the more peaceful sight of the arrival by guests on horseback, by stage, private coach, bicycle (with honeymooners mounted on tandems — the "bicycles built for two" of song and story), railway and, of course, of late years by bus and automobile by the hundreds.

Among the guests were Presidents Cleveland, McKinley, Theodore Roosevelt and Calvin Coolidge. Mrs. Calvin Coolidge was the first to sign the new guest book put into use in 1935. Franklin D. Roosevelt, when a student at Harvard, spent a weekend in Lenox visiting a young lady there. One evening they drove over to the *Red Lion* for dinner. It was a lovely moonlight night and they did not hurry their return trip to Lenox with the result that the young lady's mother became worried and sent out a searching party for the young couple who were out until the terribly late hour, for those days, of eleven o'clock! Henry W. Longfellow was another noted guest, registering at the Inn on July 26, 1860.

The items in the collection at the Inn are too numerous to mention in detail here but among the most interesting is the large mahogany table in the lobby which was originally the dining room table at the old Union League Club of New York, from which many famous men, including Dickens, Thackeray and Abraham Lincoln had eaten. Concealed in wooden boxes disguised as Bibles are a shaving brush which belonged to Daniel Webster and an old pitch pipe which was probably used by some early music teacher or song leader. In the days of the Puritan influence, shaving equipment and musical instruments were regarded as works of the Evil One and those who were bold enough to use them had to find means such as the above to keep them from prying eyes.

An appropriate ending to this necessarily abridged story of the *Red Lion Inn* and the many attractions in its vicinity, would seem to be three stanzas from a poem written in 1951, as a tribute to the Inn, by the Rev. Alfred B. Starrett, rector of St. Paul's Church, Stockbridge, with, as he wrote, "minor apologies to Edgar Guest." Another, longer, verse not quoted here referred to the Treadway family, keepers of the Inn, also to some of the other features of interest locally — Tanglewood, the Stockbridge Players, Ted Shawn's dancers and the beautiful Berkshire Hills.

It takes a heap of living in an Inn to make it right,
A heap of sun and shadow, both the sad days and the bright.
It takes a lot of caring for the welfare of the guests
To know, before they ask you, how to answer their requests.
It's not the chairs and tables nor the shingles on the roof,
But the wanting others happy that furnishes the proof.
A real Inn can't be bought, or built, or made up in a minute,
To make an Inn there's got to be a heap of living in it.
The singing and the laughter have to work into the wood,
And stoves get used to cooking so that meals are downright good.
The staff must fit together as a smoothly working whole.
Through the long cooperation there of every single soul.
You need good beds and linens, and a lovely village too,
But the things that really matter are the old things, not the new;—
The age-old smile of welcome and the well-worn wish to please,
The years of long experience that puts a guest at ease,
The gracious hospitality for travelers who roam,
And the long familiarity that makes folk feel at home.

Signboard of Colonial days from Becket in the Berkshires, now in the collection of the Connecticut Valley Historical Museum at Springfield, Massachusetts. Originally on the "Dewey House" which was burned, it was hung in such a way that it was not lost in the fire. Michael McNerney who occupied the farmhouse built on the site, treasured the signboard and preserved it from the elements. Later, it came into the possession of Frank A. Schlesinger, Executive Vice President of the Springfield Fire and Marine Insurance Company, who presented it to the Connecticut Valley Historical Museum in the name of the heirs of Michael McNerney and himself.

Courtesy of Frank A. Schlesinger,
Springfield, Massachusetts

EAGLE HOUSE
Haverhill, Massachusetts

Courtesy of Nicholas C. Johnson

THE ORIGINAL STRUCTURE was built by James Duncan one of the most prominent merchants of the town and ancestor of the well known James Duncan Phillips of Topsfield. In 1819 the property came into the possession of Col. William H. Brown who, after making various changes and improvements in the old building conducted it as a tavern from 1819 to 1872. With the addition of 75 rooms in 1853 or '54 it became one of the most comfortable and modern taverns of the time in this part of the country. It was widely known for its fish dinners. Col. Brown always made it a point to secure the first salmon taken from the Merrimack River each year to tickle the palates of his patrons. After the death of Colonel Brown the establishment changed hands several times until in 1911 it was decided to tear it down. The *Eagle House* boasted of a "roasting jack" which hung in one of its large fireplaces. It was considered at the time a most remarkable invention for it could be wound up and kept turning before the fire until the meat was done.

James Duncan had a remarkable career from his beginning as a pack-peddler, starting out from Londonderry, New Hampshire, about the year 1746 and later becoming a storekeeper and merchant interested and involved in large enterprises. His substantial progress came after he moved to Haverhill about

1747. Within a few years he owned a store of his own and as he prospered he built the mansion later to become the *Eagle House*. In due course, he became a ship owner and a substantial exporter and importer. Transactions in real estate also added to his fortune. In turn, in early records, he is recorded as "trader," "shopkeeper," "merchant," and finally he retired with the status of "gentleman." He was also active in public service and at one time served as Town Clerk of Haverhill. He was exempt from military service, probably because he had only one eye. However, he was one of the founders of the town's first Fire Club which was the name given the group organized to combat the perils of fire. When the Revolution drew on he was an ardent supporter of the cause and two of his sons were among the members of the Artillery Company organized in Haverhill in 1774. His son and namesake was taken into partnership and the firm became known as James Duncan & Son with stores in Lebanon and Haverhill, New Hampshire, and counting rooms and insurance offices in Newburyport and Boston.

James Duncan, Jr. in 1793 was one of the incorporators of the Concord-Chester-Haverhill stagecoach line as well as of the Chester Turnpike. Nathaniel Saltonstall, great, great grandfather of the present Senator Leverett Saltonstall, was another signer of the petition for the charter for a turnpike road from Concord via Chester to the Massachusetts line at Plaistow. The announcement of the opening of the stagecoach line between Concord and Haverhill stated that the citizens of the town through which the coaches would pass had agreed to lend their friendly aid in repairing roads and making them better. Also, the friendship of all teamsters was solicited to the end that they would be so obliging as to stop their teams, when they heard the stagecoach coming, so the coach might pass as the road in many places was so narrow that it was impossible to turn out with four horses and a carriage without danger of damaging the coach. It was stated that stage horses would wear bells to distinguish them from other conveyances.

HORSE MARINE NEWS

THIS INTRIGUING and amusing subject was first brought to our attention by Charles H. P. Copeland, Curator of Maritime History at the Peabody Museum of Salem, Massachusetts. By way of explanation it should be said that during the War of 1812, when the New England seacoast was virtually blockaded and when coasting commerce had practically stopped, it was thought safer to transport commodities by wagon to destinations along the New England coast. Passengers were also carried in many different kinds of wagons and coaches, which gives us an excuse for including this chapter. The *Salem Gazette*, from which these notices were taken, was a strong Federalist newspaper and articles at this time, many of them under the heading of "Jeffersonian Commerce," even spoke of "Madison's War," ridiculing the Administration at every opportunity. The people of that town also were enraged to think of materials being transported by wagon instead of by coasters and the *Salem Gazette* chose this as one way to criticize. Moreover, not contented with mere disapproval the paper printed continual headlines, "The Road to Ruin." The reason for this temporary make-shift, in the delivery of goods — namely, the embargo, brought forth these few lines in the local newspaper:

> That fatal scourge, Embargo,
> Has come upon our land;
> The Merchants' ships and cargo,
> In jeopardy do stand.

In place of the usual shipping news and occasionally by way of addition, the *Gazette* announced in nautical terms the arrivals and departures of vehicles throughout New England. These accounts are couched in such amusing terms that parts of them are quoted, some of which were given us by Mr. Copeland and the rest were found by examining the semiweekly editions during the year of 1813.

The first notice appeared on October 8 of 1813, announcing the arrival of the —

> . . . horse ship *Dare-All*, Capt. Edgerly, from a southern voyage. Parted from her consort, the *Terrapin* . . . at Danvers . . . An act of *piracy* was committed on board the latter, the captain's trunk being broken open, and 1200 dollars in bank notes stolen from it. A passenger has been taken up on suspicion, and, after an examination, before Mr. Justice Lincoln, committed to the prison ship in Worcester Harbor.

Out-of-state readers will realize the point of this remark when told that Worcester is an inland city. The same edition reported the arrival of:

> . . . the 3 horse ship *Dreadnought*, Capt. David Allen, 16 days from New York . . . with starch and drugs to Secomb & Williams . . . Spoke, near latitude of Weathersfield, the *Crispin*, Friend Alley, master, from N. York homeward bound to Lynn, but detained and waiting for trial for breach of Sabbath. (We since learn the friend Alley was condemned in heavy damages and costs of court, and was getting under weigh again.) The *Perserverance* experienced very boisterous weather during her long and toilsome passage, lost one horse, and was obliged to shift part of her cargo on board a smaller vessel; and notwithstanding its exposure, in open sea, the whole arrived 'in good order and well conditioned.' Much praise is due to the Captain for the great care, skill and fortitude with which he managed the property committed to his charge, in this trying voyage.

A few days later the 3 horse ship *Dreadnought* cleared "with all her canvas spread" with a cargo of vitriol and "cremor tartar" (cream of tartar). Another convoy of wagons arrived — bound for Charleston, S. C. "saw no cruisers, but was boarded in the offing by the 'Spectre of Hard Times' and suffered to proceed."

From the Port of Kennebunk, on October 16, came the news that there passed 20 sail of Horse and Ox Wagons, from Bath and Portland for Boston. Later in the month " . . . a large fleet of Jefferson's land ships passed by, in ballast, . . . having discharged their cargoes at the Port of Boston. The headmost was a magnificent first rate Pennsylvania-built vessel, moved by the power of 5 full-fed, stout bodied horses." Mr. Copeland informs me that this refers to a conestoga wagon and the "first rate" is a nautical term meaning a 120 gun ship-of-the-line, the largest type of vessel then constructed. The same edition contained the report of arrival in Boston of the "tandem Philadelphia pilot boat built, gig *Scramble*, Capt. Splash, from a three weeks' cruise in Rhode Island and Connecticut. She came to at about 5 P.M." Towards the last of the month the 4 horse ship *Speedwell* sailed as a transport, having on board about 5000 of the Crispin regiment of foot (5000 pairs of shoes).

Another notice read:

From 21–28 October 44 land ships took in India cargoes . . . were brought to by the revenue cutters in passing the port of Boston . . . overhaulings (of packages) were supposed to proceed without further injury, except the Administration's d . . ns for not proving good prizes.

On the 2nd of November appeared this notice:

Pawtucket Bridge, dead to windward, saw 2 four horse wagons, standing abreast, upon their larboard tacks, head towards us . . . hove about immediately, but owing to our leader missing stays, fell afoul of the starboard fore.

At Weathersfield a vessel was boarded from a Government cutter. A prize master was put on board, who ordered them to the first tavern, whereupon, after paying the innkeeper's fee, they were released. On the following day the convoy came across a man rather the worse for wear lying under the "lee of a fence" and "from his rolling," they "judged him deficient in ballast, with too much heavy stowage between decks . . . "

In early November there reached Salem a "remarkably fast sailing, new tandem-rigged, Baltimore pilot-boat-built, coppered and copper-fastened Jersey-wagon *Dash* from Vermont Bay."

The last notice we have seen was dated November 23. A passenger from Bath to Portland passed through Salem in the ship *Constitution*, drawn by 4 white horses. The log book read in part:

At half past 10 AM left port with a stiff N.E. breeze; . . . two miles W. of Bath, spoke with *Witchcraft*, from Salem, with an American burgee flying forward in Co. with the *Gerrymander*, each drawn by two horses, and bound with livestock for the privateer ship *America*. Several down with rum fever. Made sail and proceeded on our course.

No more *Horse Marine News* was discovered after the year 1813 but our informant told us that the danger of the capture of our vessels was not in any way lessened. During 1813 the matter of capture was treated to a certain extent jocosely, but in the following year proved to be a grim reality which could not be treated as a joking matter. This explains the reason for the absence of any news of this kind during 1814.

It was some years later before the commerce situation changed much for the better, as shown in these lines:

A SHIP COMES IN
(Salem 1830)

From Java, Sumatra, and old Cathay
    Another ship is home today.
Now in the heat of the noonday sun
    They are unloading cinnamon,
And even here in Town House Square
    The pungent fragrance fills the air . . .
Oh, nothing is quite so exciting to me
    As a ship just home from the China Sea.
So I will go down to the harbor soon
    And stand around all afternoon.
                                   — Oliver Jenkins

PUBLICK HOUSE
Sturbridge, Massachusetts

THE SIGNBOARD BEARS THE NAME of Col. Ebenezer Crafts, the first proprietor of this coaching tavern, established in 1771. It was appropriate to picture him on horseback for he served as a cavalry officer of a company which he equipped and drilled to join General Washington at Cambridge in 1775. Following the evacuation of that town, Crafts returned to Sturbridge and shortly after was elected Colonel of a Worcester cavalry regiment, and later commanded his own company in Shays's Rebellion.

Crafts was born in Pomfret, Connecticut and graduated from Yale in 1759. He was successful as a tavern keeper and showed excellent business ability in a number of ways. In 1790 he sold his Sturbridge property and moved to Vermont, where he founded the town of Craftsbury. The *Publick House* is proud to perpetuate his name on its signboard and elsewhere.

A mile away is Old Sturbridge Village, a living museum of early Yankee arts and crafts, which has been developed so successfully by Mr. and Mrs. George B. Wells, the former having served as head of the American Optical Company for a number of years. His father, Albert, and his uncle, Cheney, also each served for over fifty years as officers. In 1936 they founded Old Sturbridge Village as a non-profit educational museum and developed it to the point where it now contains some 50 authentic colonial buildings. The Wells family, which has contributed so much time and money to the enterprise, decided that New England's largest "living" museum rightfully belonged to the people whose heritage it represents. In 1953 the Village was transferred to the control of a public trust in ceremonies conducted there. Governor Christian A. Herter of Massachusetts accepted the property on behalf of the people of New England.

One of the prominent features of the Village is the Levi Lincoln Mansion presented in 1951 by Minott M. Rowe on behalf of the Worcester Mutual Fire Insurance Company of which he is President. The structure was moved from Worcester to the main entrance of the Village where it carries on its traditional role of hospitality established generations ago when it was the home of Levi Lincoln, the first President, in 1823, of the Insurance Company which made this distinguished and appropriate gift.

From a woodcut of 1855   *The Bettmann Archive*

MAIL COACH CHANGING HORSES

Photographed by George M. Cushing, Jr.   Courtesy of owner, J. Harold Marriott

THE GROTON INN, GROTON, MASSACHUSETTS
The part of the building in the left foreground is very much as it was in early days.

GROTON INN

ON A RECENT visit to the *Groton Inn*, the owner and manager, J. Harold Marriott, produced several letters written by James R. Joy of New York, who usually spends his summer months at this quiet, comfortable old inn. In one note he mentions a ball that was given in Groton by a Harvard student during the winter of 1823–4. A description of this entertainment, which may have been held in the tavern itself or at least used as a spill-over for the guests, was written by William Amory in 1883, sixty years after the event was held, and published, together with other letters, by Samuel A. Green, Historian of Groton and indeed of most of Massachusetts. This information is contained in a rather rare book loaned to us by Mrs. Robert M. May, Curator of the Groton Historical Society, formerly the home of George A. Boutwell, Governor of Massachusetts, and once Secretary of the Treasury. Amory explains the reason for his being in Groton at that time. It seems that half the class of 1823 at Harvard was dismissed from college in consequence of a "rebellion." (This "rebellion" of 1823, the fifth up to that year, was caused by the dissatisfaction of the students of that class, who protested by many rowdy acts against the Faculty, who retaliated by expelling forty-three out of seventy students. Reforms were insisted upon which took effect under the laws of 1825. The first "rebellion" was brought about owing to poor butter.)

Amory's account well describes a country dance of that period and we believe it would be worthwhile to mention certain of the formalities.

He first speaks of the early conveyances of that time:

. . . I remember seeing, sometimes, a coach from some distant place in New Hampshire or Vermont, on the Connecticut River, tardily arriving, some half-hour late, at the tavern in Groton, where the impatient passengers fretted and scolded the driver for keeping them waiting. He, however, with uniform plausibility, excused himself by laying the blame on the absent owners of the stage, the lameness of the horses, the badness of the road, or some stereotype accident.

The narrator then continues:

In the month of January, when the days were short and the sleighing good, I attended a grand ball at the town or tavern hall, which was densely crowded with belles and beaux from all the region round about to the distance of ten miles; who, taking advantage of good sleighing and a full moon, in every description of vehicle on runners, arrived about five o'clock in the afternoon, and kept it up in frolicsome style by dancing all night in every variety of dance then in vogue in the country, till about five o'clock the next morning, when seemingly without fatigue and as fresh as ever on the breaking up of the ball, the company in their various vehicles returned to their several homes, where most of them arrived, I suppose before mid-day.

The custom of that day of securing a partner for a dance is then described. Each gentleman and each lady drew a number and then these two had to dance together. As the narrator adds, he would naturally have rather chosen his own partner. Amory continues:

This was my experience, when, much to my horror, a tall lady, but by no means pretty, and with an awful squint, placed herself opposite to me. Happily, this chance acquaintance was only a silent partnership, imposing no obligation on either party to speak to the other . . . My *senior* partner, however, by the obliquity of her vision, had detected, without my suspicion, my disappointment at my lot; and, crossing over with an air and in a tone of offended dignity, said, 'I guess you don't like dancing, do you?' to which inquiry I made answer with all the suavity I could muster, 'Yes, I do. What makes you think I don't?' Then came the orders to 'All round,' 'Cross over,' 'Down the middle,' 'Up again' and 'Cast off' followed in military precision by a few, and by the utter confusion of all the rest.

Amory adds:

These remarks on the ball at Groton sixty years ago are not designed to reflect on the society of your native town, which I highly appreciated.

The Historical Society in Groton has an invitation to another party, a New Year's ball, held at the "Hall of Mr. Joseph Hoar," the owner of the Inn in the year 1832, the "dancing to commence at 4 o'clock." The Committee was made up of Samuel Dana, Jr., Thomas Hartwell, Thomas A. Staples and Benjamin F. Lawrence. This same Society also has in its possession the Register of this inn from 1857 to 1863 when it was known as the Central House. At this time the Proprietor was J. Nelson Hoar and the managers were his three daughters. A good description of this inn and the three managers was written by a Mrs. Delano A. Goddard in a letter from Groton to the *Worcester Daily Spy* in 1876, after giving an account of the celebration on the Fourth of July:

I cannot leave Groton without one word for its "Central House," its only tavern; a long, low building, with a picturesque piazza its whole length, covered with a luxuriant woodbine. It is unique, and is kept by three sisters (the Misses Hoar), who receive their visitors hospitably and serve them themselves; who, in spite of all their household duties, never seem hurried, are always to be found, always courteous, always ready. They are admirable representatives of the intelligent, capable, attractive New England girls who don't know what shirking is, but who take up the life they find waiting for them, and make of it the best thing they can.

The earliest landlord, Captain Jonathan Keep, created quite an unpopular sensation by proclaiming this place as a temperance house and as the inn pamphlet describes the situation thus created, "these lusty men of the rein voiced their disgust in no uncertain terms." This happened during the latter part of the Revolution. The brothers Hall took the house over in 1798 and were succeeded by Joseph Hoar; Henry Lawrence was later a landlord. The oldest part of the inn (the southern section) was built for Rev. Samuel Dana, who was forced to resign as he showed strong Tory tendencies.

The most noticeable object in the building today is the old and quaint German clock which was brought here from Germany by Captain Jonathan Keep, who in turn, placed it in its present location when he built the Inn during the summer of 1770. The clock has been in continuous operation since its installation at the Inn; the present James Lawrence well remembers that it played a waltz in some miraculous manner. Time, however, has caused the music to tire.

Another point of interest is a poem composed by George A. Boutwell. Upon inquiry of the present owner, it seems that the author, already mentioned as a very leading citizen, became so homesick for his Groton home while making a long visit to Paris, that he wrote some lines, a stanza of which is here quoted:

> And there still stands the inn, now old-fashioned and quaint,
> Where refreshment and comfort the traveller faint
> Receives as of yore, but without the potations
> Which at times did divert the past generations.

A writer about the Inn declares that there are "bits to hint of the romance and life of the years that have gone by, and over you there will steal a spirit of peace."

The author of this chapter was kindly taken by Mrs. Robert M. May to view the old coach owned by Miss Betty Dumaine which is now kept in the barn of her estate on the outskirts of the town centre. It has seen much travel along the Great Road between Eastern Massachusetts and parts of New Hampshire and Vermont, and it may have been one of the stages that left the tavern for Boston. This old vehicle was once the property of the Lawrence family, who lived nearby in a fine old Colonial house, which might be termed a mansion. W. C. Cousins of the Aetna Life Insurance Company of Hartford writes that he has several interesting passenger lists of the stage that ran from Groton to Boston.

BUCKMAN TAVERN
Lexington, Massachusetts

THIS HISTORIC BUILDING is located just off Lexington Green — the Common where the battle of April 19th, 1775 took place — and across the street from the fountain with its statue of a minuteman which faces the line of approach of the British on that eventful day. It is now the property of the town but leased to the Lexington Historical Society which has equipped it for museum purposes and community work.

According to an interesting paper read before that Society by Edward P. Bliss on December 13, 1887, the tavern was built by Benjamin Muzzey, owner of the land, who was licensed in 1693 to keep a public house. In it was the first store and, in 1812, the first Post Office in Lexington.

John Buckman was the landlord on that famous 19th of April, 1775. Then thirty years of age, he was a member of Captain Parker's Company and his tavern was the rendezvous of the minutemen for the expected encounter. He died in 1792. Little seems to be known about him except that he was a jovial man and fond of a joke. One evening an old toper brought with him a few pennies to buy rum to take home. The landlord, remarking that he supposed the old fellow would rather have his rum than anything else in the world, was answered that nothing could induce him to give up the bottle he was taking home with him. The customer started away with his purchase. It was a dark night and he lived back on the Concord road. Buckman grabbed a candlestick that had a contrivance which snapped like the click of a pistol and followed the man to the most lonesome spot on his homeward way and then, suddenly clicking the candlestick, put the cold metal to the neck of the terrified man, demanded everything he had with him and got the rum back. That was a fine story to tell for a few days. However, shortly afterwards the prankish tavern keeper was arrested and fined $50. for highway robbery!

Joshua Simonds came into possession of the tavern on the death of Buckman and in 1794 sold it to Rufus Merriam, his son-in-law, on condition that he should keep it as a public house. Before consenting, the younger man brought his children to sleep there for a night to see if they could endure the noise. Apparently they could as he took over the inn. He had the date 1794 painted on the sign. His business consisted more in providing meals for stagecoach passengers than in furnishing lodgings, and he preferred trade with the "carriage-folk," as he expressed it, to that with teamsters. Many balls and parties were given here and on one notable occasion a fashionable group from Boston engaged the house and grounds for a day to celebrate the close of the War of 1812, erecting a marquee, or tent, for dancing. The ladies were served a fine dinner by themselves at the tavern, but the gentlemen had to provide for themselves in neighboring hostelries. There was a guard stationed around the grounds to exclude Lexington people!!

In those early days New England rum was the common drink, sold at three to five cents a glass. "Flip" was a popular drink made of home-brewed beer, sugar and a dash of Jamaica rum, stirred in a mug with a red-hot iron, called a "loggerhead," which made the beverage boil and foam and gave it a burnt, bitter flavor. When a group was seated before the fire one great mug was passed around. It was such a favorite concoction in the winter time that the loggerhead was always kept handy in the fire.

It is probable that few towns in New England suffered a greater change than befell Lexington with the coming of the railroad. Prior to that period eleven taverns in the town were none too many and their accommodations were taxed to a degree which would not be endured by travelers of this day. Two beds in a room and two lodgers to a bed was the rule.

The customary charge for lodging in half a bed was ten cents, later raised to twelve and a half cents. That's when prices began to rise in this country! Breakfast and supper were each twelve and a half cents, while dinner was commonly twenty-five cents. Horses were put up for fifty cents, but they were well fed and grain was costly.

The tavern keepers were mostly farmers and always large buyers of the produce of their neighbors. Hay and grain sold at good prices which meant much to the farmers in New England. Great wagons, either horse or ox-drawn, laden with grain, piled with wooden ware or packed with homespun woolens or other products of the farms of New Hampshire and Vermont moved along the highways on the way to the Boston market. Some thrifty drivers brought fodder for their horses and a box of food for themselves, paying only ten cents for lodging and, of course, something for the common drink, New England rum. Although there was much liquor consumed, there was very little drunkenness as the good sense of the people of the country led them to be temperate in their use of intoxicants. Though the farmers who stopped at the taverns left comparatively little money there, they were always welcome and gridirons were hung about the bar-room fireplaces for their free use in warming the food they brought with them. Some of the drivers passing through Lexington came from as far away as Canada. In addition to the wagon loads of produce, droves of cattle, sheep and hogs and flocks of turkeys used the highways and were kept overnight in the tavern yards, or some place nearby. It is easy to understand why many of the farmers, drovers and tavern keepers dreaded the coming of the railroads and accused them of bringing ruin to the country, just as all new forms of transportation met with opposition in their turns.

MUNROE TAVERN
Lexington, Massachusetts

WILLIAM MUNRO, JR. built this tavern in 1695, and the next year he was licensed to keep a public house which remained in the family until 1730. William's father had been taken prisoner by Cromwell's soldiers at the battle of Worcester and deported to Boston. He settled in Lexington, then known as Cambridge Farms, about the year 1660.

A grandson of the original builder and owner of this tavern, also named William, but with an "e" added to the Munro, purchased the property and reopened it as a public house in 1770, and it remained under the ownership of the family until 1910 when it was given to the Lexington Historical Society by the two remaining brothers.

The original sign of the tavern, decorated by a picture of a punch bowl, reproduced here, was made of a single wide board of hard white pine and hung outside the tavern on that famous April 19th of 1775. The wood in the building is early native white pine (similar to that used in our Trust Department which arouses much favorable comment) and throughout the interior are hand-hewn timbers put together with wooden pins. The chimney is of bricks made locally in 1694 and originally laid with clay mortar. The original front door of 1775, on each side of which were two windows with small panes, is now the shed door. The door to the garret is one of the old 1695 doors, but most of the other inside doors are of the period of 1860 when the tavern became a residence. Peat was used as a fuel in the early days which probably accounts for the fact that the fireplaces are smaller than in many old houses.

The "Earl Percy Room" was the name of the dining room in the tavern because of the fact that when Earl Percy reached Lexington on the afternoon of April 19, 1775, with reinforcements of 1000 men and two cannons, he made the hostelry his headquarters. This room was also used as a temporary hospital at the time of the historic encounter which is an outstanding part of our American tradition. In the ceiling of the tap room, where the British soldiers were freely supplied with liquor, is a hole made by a bullet from one of their muskets. There is also a "Washington Room" so named because boniface Colonel Munroe cleared a bedchamber to provide a private dining room for the President when, during his journey through New England, he visited Lexington on November 5, 1789.

Some time after 1770 an ell was built on the northwest side of the house, the upper floor of which was a hall in which balls and parties were held. This addition, the upper floor of which could be used as sleeping quarters when business was extra brisk, was removed in 1860 when the tavern was converted to a home. The Hiram Lodge of Free Masons was organized in the hall which was long used as a lodge room.

Jonas Munroe succeeded his father, William, as landlord and enjoyed the highest prosperity of tavern-keeping days until the railroads turned away the course of travelers. His inn was always a homelike and inviting place, the doors of which were never locked. In fact, the tavern was a hospitable public home for townspeople as well as for strangers.

The visit of President George Washington was, of course,

one of the outstanding events in the life of the Tavern. We are grateful to Edwin B. Worthen, President of the Lexington Savings Bank, who brought to our attention Volume I of the Proceedings of the Lexington Historical Society, published by that organization in 1890. This provided much information which we believe is not too widely known concerning this momentous day. The visit took place during Washington's journey into New England which began at New York on Thursday, October 15, 1789, in his first year as President.

Washington had planned to visit Lexington on October 26th but because he was suffering from a cold contracted when he was waiting for his official reception to Boston to get started, he was obliged to change his plans and defer his visit to a later date. In spite of his cold and an inflamed eye, he had tea with Governor Hancock that evening at the latter's home where he enjoyed the fragrant beverage in the Governor's beautiful china, of which Hancock was very proud.

After visiting Cambridge, Lynn, Salem, Marblehead and Portsmouth, N. H., he headed back for Exeter, N. H., and pushed on to Haverhill, Mass., where he spent the night. At sunrise the next morning he left for Andover where he breakfasted at *Abbot's Tavern*, meeting with much attention from Judge Samuel Phillips. His diary mentions that "Mr. Phillips accompanied me through Billariki to Lexington where I dined and viewed the spot on which the first blood was spilt on the 19th April, 1775. Here I parted with Mr. Phillips and proceeded to Watertown, 8 miles. We lodged at the house of a Widow Coolidge near the bridge and a very indifferent house it is."

Fortunately, we have available excerpts from an eye-witness story about the President's dinner in Lexington given in a letter from Miss Sarah Munroe, daughter of the landlord, to her friend, Miss Mary Mason, in New York. "We have had great doings here. Our Loved President has journied here to Lex. & has took dinner at our very House." Then she goes on to tell about the bustle in the kitchen in preparing, with the help of neighbors, "Pyes and pudings" for the great day ahead. They sat up all night watching the oven "lest some mischance befal the contents." Unfortunately this took place the day and night before the President was first expected to visit Lexington! When word came that because of his "infloowenza" he had to postpone that visit, the neighbors were invited to "come eat the President his Feast." The same agitated performance took place before the actual arrival of the great man on November 5, 1789. This time the young lady adds "the Brewwing of a fresh Lot of beer for the Flip" to the cooking activities. All the plate was scoured, the brasses rubbed and the floors sanded. Clothes were pressed and starched, but with it all they did not deem it necessary to stay up all night to watch the oven. When the time came for the President to arrive, all who could be spared went out to watch and welcome him. "Betimes Mr. Washington appered, bestridding a most hansome White horse. He wore a millitary Habit, much like my Worthy Father, only gayer and with fine things, I mind not what they call 'em, on the showlders. His Hat he wore under his arm and he bent himself to the one side and the other as he Passed. I promise you we huzzared stoutly, but he bowed not, only leaned, as one shd say, towards us." Then the observant young lady mentions those who "road" with the President, including Mr. Phillips, "the Worshippfull President of the Sennate." Over at the Meeting House stood all the great men of the town, including those who were in the famous fight of April 19th, to greet the honored guest "exsepting my Father who could not be spar'd from the House." She mentions that one of the veterans had his arm in a sling, "tho' 'twas well, years agone." One of the men went up to hold the President's stirrup but he would not allow that service and "threw himself from the sadle with a Jump, for 'tis said he is wonderus strong tho' so old." (Washington was 57 at the time!) After the customary speeches had been made the group went to the spot where blood was spilled and our young lady reporter records that "Mr Washington seemed somthing sollem at first, but soon waxed livlyer and asked many Questions, they told me, of the Fight. He would, moreover, see the Houses round about, and when he enterred Mr Buckman his Tavern, I was in great figget 'till he come out, fearing lest Mr Merriam who is but just approbbated as a taverner and knows nought about the Bisness, might entreat him into Eating *there.*" At last the hour of dining, 2 o'clock, neared and all converged on the *Munroe Tavern.* "There stood my Father and step-mother at the tap-room Door . . . My Father looked grandly in his rejimentels and proud indeed was I of him as he led the way to the Dinner-room prepar'd for Mr Washington in the upper room." The meal was described in detail: "rosted Beef, a showlder of pork, Chickins, pyes, Puddings, Syllybubs, and, best of all, some fine young Pigens sent in by the Widow Mulliken. Mr Washington would have none but plane things, however, saying, as my Father handed the others to him, 'That is to good for me.' When the pigens, of which there was but few, were served, the Prest said 'Are all these fine kickshores (kickshaws) for my servents to?' My Father stamering that he had not tho't to give them Such, his Highness bade the dish of Squobs be divided in half that his Black men, forsooth, might have the same as him." Miss Munroe then retails the table conversation which covered among other things the "Vilenes of the Roads, calling them as Blind and Ignorent as the directions of the Inhabittents." She thought he had more to say than was seemly about the ladies "how hansome he found them, their black Hair being to his liking." Apparently our first President was one gentleman who didn't prefer blondes! The young lady's eagle eye noted that Washington was exceed- ingly frugal in his drinking as well as in his eating, as he took but one mug of beer and two glasses of wine during the whole meal. She states that "after the second Glass he rellated sundry Aneckdotes, but with such gravyty & slowness that none durst smile." He told his dinner companions that Benjamin Franklin had been much vexed in England when the British complained that the Yankees took advantage of them on the 19th of April by firing from behind stone walls. Franklin's retort was "Were there not two sides to the walls?" The next story she records may not be amusing to some Yale men, but we're mentioning it as a matter of history. Washington told of coming to a tavern one night when the host was away and where they awoke his wife. On hearing the President was below seeking shelter she would have naught to do with him, "believing him to be but the President of the little Yale Colledge in Connt." Washington also talked of farming matters and had much to ask about the crops, etc. remarking that he thought the hogs in New England had unusually long legs. This remark "well-nigh upsett the comp'y . . . and the mirth might have prov'd Unbecoming had not just then arose a great cracking and howling." This timely interruption brought the dinner to a close. It proved to be caused by two of the younger Munroe children, Jonas and Lucinda, who had climbed into a buttonwood tree to watch the proceedings through a window. The limb on which they were perched snapped and Jonas caught the frill of Lucinda's skirt and held her, loudly bawling, dangling in mid-air. Before the diners could reach the scene of the accident, one of Washington's servants had rescued the little girl from her perilous position. Shortly afterward the party broke up and the President entered his carriage to take his departure for Watertown, declining a mug of flip which Host Munroe offered him. We are told, however, that his companions and servants accepted this "one for the road." Miss Munroe closed her fine, newsy letter with "I have burned 3 Dips, which is sinfull, & have set up long beyond Bell-ringing to send you this, so now must I stop." Posterity is certainly indebted to her for this thorough and interesting account of one of Lexington's big events.

❧

PISTOL ORNAMENTATION
of Stagecoach Days

IT MIGHT be of interest to our readers to know how we happened to run across the sidelight on the old stagecoach days, portrayed on the opposite page.

In November of 1952 a news item in the *Boston Globe* about a burglary in a suburb of Boston reported that the only article missing was an antique Colt revolver. There was nothing particularly unusual about that, but we were then working on the first volume of *Taverns and Stagecoaches of New England*, and when the description further mentioned that the imprint of a stagecoach appeared on the stolen firearm we thought it merited investigation. It turned out that the revolver was never recovered, but the victim of the robbery informed us that the Boston Police Department, in trying to identify the lost article, had shown him a similar one, so he was sure we would find one at Police Headquarters. Through the courtesy of Police Commissioner, Colonel Thomas F. Sullivan, we found that in the early 1850's Samuel Colt had issued an advertising sheet illustrating this type of revolver which he manufactured in Hartford, Connecticut. Correspondence with Colt's Manufacturing Company revealed that there was a fine copy of this advertising sheet in their extensive museum, and a photograph of it was provided us for use here. This seemed more effective than trying to photograph the decoration on the revolver itself. Mr. D. W. Hayward, Secretary of Colt's Manufacturing Company, called our attention to the fact that the engraving on the Navy Model — which was also used by the Army — is particularly interesting because the engagement pictured is an encounter between the Texas Navy and the Mexican fleet in 1843 when Texas was an independent nation.

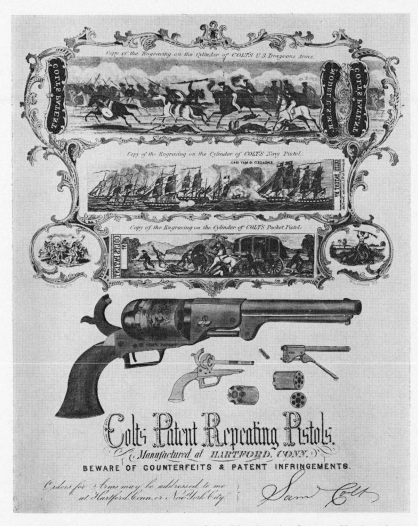

Courtesy of Colt's Manufacturing Company, Hartford, Conn.

A COLT ADVERTISING SHEET OF ABOUT 1850

While only the illustrations of the pistol and the engraving immediately above it are pertinent to this brochure, the other two seem interesting enough to reproduce also. The engraving of the Navy model — which was also used by the Army — is of special interest because the engagement pictured is an encounter in 1843 between the Texas Navy and the Mexican fleet at the time when Texas was an independent nation. The illustrations are apparently a combination of three engravings used in transferring the designs to the cylinders and, therefore, the lettering on the ends shows in reverse.

The old posting song, variously known as "Who's for the Coach Tonight," "The Postilion," and "Bristol Town," was called to our attention by George L. Moore, previously mentioned, and later two slightly differing versions were found in the *Boston Sunday Globe* in the section entitled "Songs and Poems of Long Ago."

The night is late, we dare not wait,
    The winds begin to blow.
An' ere we gain the hollow plain,
    there'll be a storm I trow.
An' as we pass the Beggar's tree,
    Look out!   The Dark Look out!
The phantom horseman you will see
He'll crack his whip and shout,
    Tra-la!   Tra-la!   Tra-la!
Who's for the coach tonight?

For we are bound for Bristol town
    before the morning light,
    Tra-la!   Tra-la!   Tra-la!
Oh, I've a wife in Bristol town,
    a wife and children three
As they are sleeping safe and sound
    But she keeps watch for me.
And who would quake, the road
    to take with such a prize in store
Then ravens croak on Hangman's rack
    as a storm be at our fore.
    Tra-la!   Tra-la!   Tra-la!
And a storm be at our fore.
Who's for the coach tonight?

For we are bound for Bristol town
    before the morning light,
    Tra-la!   Tra-la!   Tra-la!
Then one glass more,
The ale is fine, a toast sweet ladies fair
To each man's home, good masters mine.
And may we soon be there
The sparks shall flash as on we dash
The clatter'n' wheels shall spin
As every sleepin' loon shall stir,
    to see the coach roll in.
    Tra-la!   Tra-la!   Tra-la!
    To see the coach roll in.
    Tra-la!   Tra-la!   Tra-la!

Courtesy Edward Dane   *Photograph by G. M. Cushing, Jr.*

Through the courtesy of Mr. Dane, President of the Brookline Trust Company, we are privileged to reproduce above what is said to be the only existing picture of the famous old *Punch Bowl Tavern* of Brookline. The original is one of Mr. Dane's prized possessions and hangs in the office of the Trust Company of which he is President.

PUNCH BOWL TAVERN
Brookline

IN 1717 James Goddard built a modest two-story hipped roof dwelling house in Brookline situated on the eastern corner of Pearl and Washington Streets, next to the present location of the Brookline Theatre. On the direct route for traffic between Boston, New York and the West, this way led over a bridge across the Muddy River built in 1640, (long since replaced, of course), and was, therefore, an almost ideal location for a tavern. John Ellis, who bought the property in 1740 realized its advantages and, after enlarging the building, he converted it into a public house which for nearly one hundred years was a famous stopping place for travelers.

There were at least two other taverns in Brookline deserving of mention — the *Dana* in Harvard Square at the junction of

Washington and Harvard Streets, and the *Richards* in Chestnut Hill on Sherburne Road (now Heath Street) where Hammond Street now crosses. However the *Punch Bowl* was by far the most popular and prosperous, to such an extent that the Brookline Village of today became known then as Punch Bowl Village and its fame was spread far and wide. As the tavern flourished financially the owners expanded it from time to time by the purchase and removal of old houses from Boston and vicinity which were added to the original structure. This resulted in a collection of a curious medley of rooms of all sorts and sizes, thus producing a new architectural order appropriately described as "conglomerate" by Miss Harriet F. Woods, whose "Historical Sketches of Brookline" was published in 1874.

The tavern and its necessary out-buildings finally occupied a frontage of several hundred feet extending from the present theatre to beyond Pearl Street, nearly to Brookline Avenue. Large elm trees shaded each end of the main building as well as the hospitable entrance and in the front yard was the tavern pump. Beneath its overhanging second story a bench was available to guests or townspeople who always gathered around to hear news of the outside world from the travelers. While details of the sign are not distinct in the illustration which accompanies this chapter, it was adorned by an overflowing punch bowl and ladle, shaded by the leaves of a fruitful lemon tree, with lemons lying beneath the tree, around the bowl.

Before and during the Revolution it was the center of the town's life. The Selectmen held meetings and annual banquets there and British officers frequented the place in large numbers. The pillory, stocks, and other features of public interest were installed near the tavern and notices of meetings and entertainments were posted on the "publishment board" nearby. The two outstanding events of the day however were the arrival of the New York and Uxbridge stagecoaches which always meant increased activity thereby attracting a lot of attention, as well as business to the tap room. As was the case with most taverns of that era, the *Punch Bowl* boasted of a ballroom which was well patronized by groups from surrounding towns. In addition to the stagecoaches many wagons made use of the highway in front of the tavern and it was not unusual to see a line of vehicles extending from the present Kent Street (then Harrison Place) to Brookline Avenue. A brook at the spot later occupied by the railroad crossing was a handy place for watering the horses, and travelers never seemed at a loss to find the liquid refreshments of their choice.

By 1827 business began to slacken and the need for the tavern rapidly diminished with the result that this interesting old building was torn down in 1833. The site is marked by a bronze plate on the Brookline Theatre, placed by the Brookline Historical Society in 1949, and it is safe to say that this famous hostelry will forever have an honored place in the history of Brookline.

We are indebted to Mr. Gorham Dana for allowing us to use much of the material from an article he wrote on the old taverns of the town for the Brookline Historical Society. The following anecdote is so unusual and amusing that we are taking the liberty of quoting it in full:

"The story is told of a notable occasion at the tavern in 1783 when Selectman Joshua Boylston, a nephew of the famous Dr. Zabdiel Boylston who first introduced inoculation for small pox into this country, attended a selectmen's dinner here. He was rather a reserved and stern man of about 55 years who had never married. Squire Sharp, the town clerk and also a bachelor, was present, and there was some bantering directed toward the two bachelors regarding marriage. When asked why he had never married, Selectman Boylston replied that he had never found any one who would take him. Abigail Baker, sister of the landlord of the inn, a cheerful trim little body of about 40 years, was waiting on table, and to the astonishment of the company remarked, 'I will have you, Mr. Boylston.' 'Squire Sharp,' said Boylston, 'Do you hear that? Publish the banns next

Sunday.' When he found that the banns had not been published he asked the Squire why. 'I thought it was all a joke,' replied the clerk. 'Publish them next week or I will prosecute,' he was told by the irate selectman. This was done, and they were married and apparently lived happily ever after.''

ళి

TABLET on the site of COOPER TAVERN, corner of Massachusetts Ave. and Medford St., Arlington Center, Massachusetts. In the Tavern, two aged men, Jabez Wyman and Jason Winship, sitting over their toddy, were killed on April 19, 1775 when the Redcoats, rushing through the town, then known as Menotomy, fired blindly through the windows.

Suggested by Jason A. Swadkins

Photograph by Dean H. Eastman

The "OLD ORDINARY"
Hingham, Massachusetts

ESTABLISHMENT OF "ordinaries" (as taverns or inns were called in the early days) for the accommodation of travelers and the use of townspeople, followed rather closely the establishment of churches in this country. The welfare of travelers and a method for regulating the sale of intoxicating liquors apparently seemed important enough for the authorities — at first the General Court and later the County courts — to recommend at first, and then to enforce, the opening of some kind of public house in each community. Sometimes land was granted; pasturage for cattle, or exemption from church rates and school taxes were inducements offered to encourage the keeping of an "ordinary." In 1656, the General Court made towns liable to a fine for not maintaining such an establishment. Concord, Mass., was one of those fined, by the way. The name "ordinary" comes from England where it was customary for eating places to have a daily "ordinary," a mid-day meal, or supper, generally a particular dish on which the host specialized, served at a common table at a fixed time.

Hingham lost little time in meeting the needs of the day as the site for the subject of this chapter was granted to Joseph Andrews on the settlement of the town in 1635, and local history claims that the main portion of the building was erected by either Joseph, or his son, Thomas Andrews. The date 1650 on its quaint sign confirms the belief that it is one of the oldest of such hostelries extant today, though the original structure is now beneath the rooftree of the present building.

A document issued in 1702 by the selectmen of the town gave Landlord Andrews permission to "sell Strong Waters on Broad Cove Lane provided he sent his customers home at reasonable hours, with ability to keep their legs." Only upright men of good standing were permitted to keep taverns in those days, as it was thought of primary importance to have law and order maintained within their walls. Both Joseph Andrews and his son Thomas were Puritans of fine character and typical of the sturdy pioneers of their day. Many restrictions controlled the activities of these early inn keepers. At times they were forbidden to have any dancing or singing on their premises. No games, such as carding, dicing, tally, bowls, billiards, slidegroat, shuffle-board, quoits, loggets and nine-pins were allowed. Some of those names of games are as curious as the names of some of the alcoholic beverages that the *Old Ordinary* dispensed, such as Calibogris, Canstantia, Kill-Devil, Rumbullion, Switchel, Ebulum, etc.

The taproom behind the parlor of the *Old Ordinary* is one of the most interesting features of the place. The wicket, which used to be triced up when refreshments were requested, is hinged to the ceiling, and the shelves are loaded with flasks, bottles and containers of all sorts, while demijohns and casks will be noted on the floor and under the bar. The writer was especially impressed years ago, on his first visit to this relic of ancient times, by the grooves worn in the floor behind the bar by generations of bartenders. While the residents of Hingham and visitors to the town may not have been heavy drinkers, apparently they were fairly steady patrons of the taproom, judging by the way that floor was worn down behind the bar. Daniel Webster, who might be considered a connoisseur on the subject, is said to have called the landlord's spiced wine the finest to be found in New England.

The people of Hingham were whole-heartedly against slavery prior to the Civil War which brought an end to that blight on our civilization. When Boston became "too hot" for William Lloyd Garrison, Wendell Phillips, Parker Pillsbury, Theodore Parker and other leaders of the anti-slavery movement, they would transfer their meetings to the *Old Ordinary* in Hingham. A most interesting account book kept by Francis Jackson,

Treasurer of the Vigilance Committee of Boston, has been reproduced by the Bostonian Society, Old State House, Boston, thereby making available to the public at a modest price an historic document which is unique and of great interest to those seeking detailed information about the work of the so-called Underground Railroad which concealed and forwarded fugitive slaves to freedom in Canada. The record book is a model of clarity and the penmanship of the Treasurer is superb. As pointed out in a pamphlet by the late Wilbur H. Siebert supplementing the Jackson book, it is very unusual to find such incriminating records as they were seldom kept, because anyone caught supporting such an unlawful movement, financially or otherwise, would have been liable to severe penalties. The whole venture was a very risky one which makes participation in it all the more creditable. Covering in detail all financial transactions from October 21, 1850, after the enactment of the Fugitive Slave Law of that year, the last entry was made in April of 1861. One of the largest collections recorded in this fascinating book was that taken in Hingham by John A. Andrew, then practicing law in Boston, later to become the Civil War Governor of our Commonwealth. His interest in Hingham was natural as he married Eliza Jones Hersey of that town, and they spent their early married life there. The total turned over to the Vigilance Committee was $102.00, entered under date of March 24, 1851, as from Rev. Oliver Stearns and others, probably collected at a meeting at the *Old Ordinary* or in Dr. Stearns' church located three doors south of the tavern. A quick examination of the book shows another entry of $30.00 from Reuben Tower, South Parish, Hingham, early in 1851. Several other "Hingham" names appear as donors, though not identified as from that town. It is interesting to note several entries showing repayment by escaped slaves of money advanced to them by the Committee. Some time later there is an entry showing a deduction of $3.25 for counterfeit money given to collectors. We are confident that it did not come from Hingham!

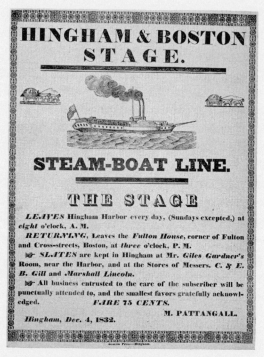

This copy of an original handbill advertising the early steamboat service between Boston and Hingham was contributed by Samuel Wakeman, General Manager of Bethlehem Steel Company's Shipbuilding Division, Quincy, Mass. Mr. Wakeman obtained the handbill in New York from a person who had picked it up in Boston. The bill is printed on thin paper and still is in good condition. Mr. Wakeman says that the advertisement probably means that the steamer connected with the stage line to Plymouth. The vessel depicted must be the old General Lincoln, which made her first Boston–Hingham trip on June 16, 1832, and continued in the service until 1844 when she was sold to New York interests.

The *Old Ordinary* has changed ownership only a few times since its establishment, but in 1750 it was enlarged to meet the increasing demands on its hospitality. On June 1st, 1923, after it had been restored, it came into possession of the Hingham Historical Society. All the work and practically all the furniture in the fine collection represent contributions by members of the Society.

Visitors to this old tavern, which is open for inspection during the summer season, will find an impressive collection of early American handiwork — bed quilts, embroidery, Sandwich glass, wooden ware, (for which Hingham was famous) furniture, etc., along with many other items used in homes and taverns in the earliest days. One of the interesting relics is the cradle in which Governor John A. Andrew was rocked as a baby. On a wall hang framed bills giving the schedule of the old stagecoach line between Boston and Hingham owned by Abiel Wilder, a descendant of one of the earliest settlers and one of the best known of the tavern's proprietors. At that time, 1825, the *Old Ordinary* was listed as Wilder's Hotel. In 1834, ownership of the stage line was given as A. & B. Wilder in Badger & Porter's "Stage Register" which then served the purpose of our time-tables of today, as mentioned in a previous chapter.

We hope this brief recital will be an inducement to our readers to plan to visit this ancient hostelry and enjoy a step backward into the atmosphere of Colonial days.

THE TREE OF KNOWLEDGE
Duxbury, Massachusetts

ONE OF THE most interesting sidelights pertaining to the carrying of the mails in the early days, first by mounted "runners" and then by stagecoaches, is the story of the "Tree of Knowledge" in the western part of Duxbury, Mass., known as Tarkiln. The unusual name of this section is derived from the fact that a tar kiln was established there to supply the tar needed to caulk vessels in days when numerous shipyards were in active operation along the shore line of Duxbury.

It seems that in the early Colonial days it was customary to leave letters and parcels at an oak tree standing at the junction of the Massachusetts Bay Path (now Route 3) and the highway running through Tinkertown. The Bay Path was the westerly of the two King's Highways laid out soon after the Plymouth and the Massachusetts Bay colonies were united. It ran from Boston through Dorchester, Quincy, Weymouth Landing, West Scituate, Hanover, Pembroke, West Duxbury and Plymouth. The easterly highway, known as the Old Coast Road, ran from Boston through Milton, Quincy, Weymouth, Hingham, Cohasset, Scituate, Marshfield, Duxbury, Kingston and Plymouth. The Duxbury road and the one through Tinkertown were not laid out until 1763, and it may be that letters or parcels were left at the tree at the crossroads to be picked up by the "runner" between Plymouth and Boston, but it could have been only a very informal arrangement. However, on May 12, 1775, the first Post Office was established at Plymouth by the Provincial Congress, with William Watson as Postmaster. Mounted mail carriers began to make regular trips in June of that year, and it was about this time that the sturdy oak tree at Tarkiln became known as the "Tree of Knowledge." A box was nailed to the

BOSTON,
Plymouth & Sandwich
MAIL STAGE,

CONTINUES TO RUN AS FOLLOWS:

LEAVES Boston every Tuesday, Thursday, and Saturday mornings at 5 o'clock, breakfast at Leonard's, Scituate ; dine at Bradford's, Plymouth ; and arrive in Sandwich the same evening. Leaves Sandwich every Monday, Wednesday and Friday mornings ; breakfast at Bradford's, Plymouth ; dine at Leonard's, Scituate, and arrive in Boston the same evening.

Passing through Dorchester, Quincy, Wyemouth, Hingham, Scituate, Hanover, Pembroke, Duxbury, Kingston, Plymouth to Sandwich. *Fare*, from Boston to Scituate, 1 doll. 25 cts. From Boston to Plymouth, 2 dolls. 50 cts. From Boston to Sandwich, 3 dolls. 63 cts.

N. B. Extra Carriages can be obtained of the proprietor's, at Boston and Plymouth, at short notice.— STAGE BOOKS kept at Boyden's Market-square, Boston, and at Fessendon's, Plymouth.

LEONARD & WOODWARD.

BOSTON, *November* 24, 1810.

Courtesy of Bostonian Society

tree for the convenience of the people of Duxbury and the surrounding neighborhood, and its fame became widespread.

From a photograph by Baldwin Coolidge   *Courtesy of E. K. R. Revere*

DOTY TAVERN
Ponkapog, Canton, Massachusetts

WHEN THE MEN of the Province of Massachusetts were enraged at the blind policy of Parliament toward America, it was decided by bold patriots that throughout the thirteen provinces "Congresses" should be held. (This term was adopted because the Regulation Act forbade the holding of town meetings except by permission of the Governor.) Suffolk County took the lead in this movement. Seeking an inland town where they would be free from interference, Samuel Adams, Dr. Joseph Warren and others agreed that Stoughton, by its geographical location, would be most appropriate for their plans. *Doty's Tavern*, (in what is now Canton), which was of good repute, kept by Colonel Thomas Doty, a patriotic officer of the militia, was selected as the place in Stoughton for the holding of the "Congress" on August 16th, 1774. A metal tablet now marks the tavern site on Washington Street, Canton, (Route 138) just south of the junction of that highway with Route 128 at the base of the

Blue Hills. Before adjournment, resolutions were adopted which were the basis of the celebrated "Suffolk Resolves," voted at a subsequent meeting, which were carried to Philadelphia by Paul Revere and approved by the Continental Congress on the 17th of September, 1774.

The tavern over which Doty presided was noted for its good cheer. The proprietor was jovial, well known and respected. He kept the best of viands, and it was said that he could mix the best glass of grog of any landlord in all the country around. His hostelry stood high in the favor of the stage drivers who were always eager to arrive there. Around his capacious hearth on winter evenings there congregated the men of the village to discuss over pipe and bowl matters of interest to their community and the Province as a whole. John Adams frequently stopped there, and other travelers added to the interest of discussions. Doty had seen a lot of service in the militia and had been on active duty with Abercrombie's army on the expedition to attack Fort Ticonderoga. After his return from the French and Indian War, during which, under Bradstreet, he had crossed Lake Ontario with his troops and captured Fort Frontenac, he was in business for a short time at Plymouth and Middleborough. In 1760 he kept the *Lamb Tavern* in Boston, moving in 1864 to Canton, then a part of Stoughton.

It was at *Doty's Tavern*, when the British fleet under Lord Howe was reported off the coast meditating a descent on Boston, that the Rev. Samuel Dunbar, the beloved second minister of the First Parish Church of Christ at Stoughton, (from which Canton was set off in 1797) prayed that God would "put a bit in their mouths, and jerk them about, send a strong northeast gale, and dash them to pieces on Cohasset Rock." Again, in a period of great anxiety he prayed that the Lord would let the enemy return to the land whence they came "for Thou knowest, O God, that their room is better than their company."

The *Doty Tavern*, which existed until December 19, 1888,

when it was destroyed by fire, was built by Major John Shepard who was a notable man in the community. As early as 1726 he was a popular tavern keeper and received from his fellow townsmen every office it was in their power to bestow. However, late in life, he became unpopular because of his treatment of the Ponkapog Indians, which led to his being expelled from the General Court.

In addition to John Adams, later to become President of the United States, many celebrities stopped at this famous old Inn. Lafayette slept beneath its roof when on his way from Taunton to Boston. In an incredibly short time the news spread that the noted Frenchman was at the tavern, and on the morning of his departure the townsfolk gathered by the roadsides to wave their good wishes as his coach proceeded on its journey.

South Boston and City
Coach

Will in future leave **MRS. PHINNEY'S COFFEE-HOUSE**, South Boston, at half past 8, and 11 o'clock, A. M. and 2, and half past 4 o'clock, P. M.

RETURNING—Leaves the **MARLBORO' HOTEL** at 10 o'clock, A. M. and at 1, 3, and 6 o'clock, P. M.

NORTON & CLARK, *Directors.*

SOUTH BOSTON, OCT. 21, 1826.

THE MORSE
and Other Early Taverns of
Walpole, Massachusetts

IT IS NOT KNOWN just when the *Morse Tavern* was built, but tradition says that at least part of it was erected more than two hundred and twenty-five years ago. In any event, there is no doubt that the tavern was in operation from early turnpike days, and it was there that Lafayette stopped in 1824 long enough for

Courtesy Charles S. Bird, Jr.

the distinguished visitor to sample David Morse's hospitality. It stood on the site of the present Triangle Building of Bird & Son, Inc., the oldest and largest industry in Walpole.

From the picture of it in its later days, reproduced here, it will be seen it was not a very imposing structure but at one time it boasted of two large wings which added much to its capacity in the days when it was on the route used by the busy stagecoach lines. In one corner was a store in which the neighbors were served rum at 4¢ a drink while the travelers patronizing it were charged 6¢ in the bar of the tavern. Walpole's first post office was located in the tavern, and on the second floor was the largest hall between Dedham and Wrentham until after 1850. Sold in 1847 and converted into stores and tenements, about three years later it was purchased by Francis W. Bird, son of George Bird, founder of Bird & Son, who offered the hall for public use without charge, except for lighting. He went further and assisted in getting speakers of note to appear there, and it is believed that it was here that Julia Ward Howe gave her first lecture. After 1884, when the new post office building was erected, the old tavern was used by Bird & Son for business purposes until it was replaced by the present building mentioned above.

It was quite natural that Mr. Bird should have been interested and influential in getting as a speaker the famous author and reformer, Julia Ward Howe, whose name is now known to millions by reason of her stirring Civil War poem set to music as "The Battle Hymn of the Republic." He had been an outstanding figure in the Anti-Slavery cause and the Free Soil Party, organizing the activities of the latter in his vicinity in 1848 and attending as a delegate the party's first State and National Conventions. Years before this he had set tongues wagging when he politely showed the negro servant of his newly-acquired bride into the family pew at the South Dedham Congregational Church before he and his wife entered. He was one of the original members of the so-called "Bird Club" which met for luncheon every Saturday at a Boston coffee house to discuss political and social matters. One of his fellow members was John A. Andrew, one of the leaders of the Vigilance Committee of Boston which ran so effectively the Underground Railroad in aid of slaves fleeing to safety in Canada and elsewhere. It is not surprising that Mr. Bird is listed as one of the contributors to the Vigilance Committee in which his friend was so active. Later he was one of those who successfully urged Andrew to enter the contest for the office of Chief Executive of our Commonwealth in which he was the winner by a substantial margin. History records that Andrew thoroughly justified the faith and enthusiasm of his supporters by making a notable record as our War Governor during the period from 1861 to 1865.

In connection with his political activities, Mr. Bird formed a friendship with Senator Charles Sumner which lasted until that great statesman's death, and naturally he was deeply moved when Sumner was assaulted and beaten into insensibility while working at his desk in the Senate Chamber in Washington. He was in the forefront of the group in Walpole which, as in many communities, passed resolutions denouncing Sumner's assailant and the slaveholders' power which he represented. When Sumner had recovered his health well enough to travel, he visited Walpole where he spoke to a capacity audience in the old Orthodox Church. This served to increase the fervor with which Bird worked for the Anti-Slavery cause. Sumner was so impressed by his friend's zeal that he once dubbed him jokingly as "Our Bird of Freedom." Mr. Bird's admiration and affection for Sumner is shown by the fact that he named his son Charles Sumner for the crusading martyr, and his grandson and great grandson still carry on the honored name.

Such a well traveled area as Walpole supported its full share of taverns of which we will mention only a few. Just south of the bridge over the Neponset at King's Bridge (or Kingsbridge), near the site of the plant of the George H. Morrill Division of the Sun Chemical Corp. in Norwood (then a part of Walpole), the *White Tavern*, kept by Henry White, did a brisk business catering to travelers. The famous old *Roebuck Tavern* was on the Post Road on the northeast corner of the present Coney Street in East Walpole. The *Brass Ball* tavern, which stood just across the Neponset River at Walpole Centre, toward Wrentham, on the northwest side of what is now West Street, was kept by Deacon

Ezekiel Robbins. There is some doubt as to how long the worthy deacon kept the tavern, but it seems sure he was in business in 1740 as it was in that year that he placed a milestone a short distance beyond his house, toward Wrentham, marking the 20-mile point from Boston. This "mill-stone near Robins pauster barrs" is mentioned in the Walpole town records of 1744 and now has a place of honor in front of the Wrentham Town Hall. In 1771 a traveling business man of New Haven, William Gregory, noted in his diary that he put up "at one Mr. Robins,' just 19½ miles from Boston." Deacon Robbins was one of Walpole's earliest benefactors as he gave the first schoolhouse and, on his death in 1772, left his considerable estate to the church and to the town's poor. One of the functionaries at the *Brass Ball Tavern* was the slave, "Jack," whose official duties were to eject visitors who became too boisterous. As part of the estate of Deacon Robbins, he became the property of the church which was charged in the Deacon's will "to take tender care of him and suitable provide for him all the remainder of his life and afford him a decent burial after his death." On one occasion the church society paid $6.00 to advertise for Jack's return when he ran away, and the records show that $163.33 was spent on his funeral, so the Deacon's wishes were faithfully followed to the end.

ISRAEL HATCH

Boston and Providence Stagecoach and Tavern Mogul

THE FIRST REGULAR stagecoach service between Boston and Providence was established in 1767 by Thomas Sabin of the latter place. Coaches left there every Tuesday, returning from Boston the following Thursday. It ran through Pawtucket and South Attleboro to North Attleboro, then through Wrentham and Walpole to Dedham and on to Boston over the "Neck." The section of road between North Attleboro and Wrentham was publicly laid out about 1751. Connecting with an old road leading from Dedham through Walpole and Wrentham toward Woonsocket, it soon replaced the Old Roebuck Road and held its own against turnpike competition.

This competition came with the incorporation on March 8th, 1802, of the Norfolk and Bristol Turnpike Corporation for the purpose of constructing a turnpike from the Court House in Dedham, Norfolk County, to the north parish meeting house in Attleboro in Bristol County. This was to be a so-called "artificial road" meaning that the material for surfacing, gravel, etc., was to be brought from some other place, to distinguish them from the "natural roads" where the surface was composed of the soil on the spot or thrown out in digging the ditches. It is said there were only three of these "artificial" turnpike roads in Massachusetts, the other two being the Newburyport and the Salem turnpikes. While requirements as to the width of the roads varied and part, at least, of the Norfolk and Bristol turnpike was supposed to be twenty-four feet wide and crowned twelve inches, old records of Lancaster, Massachusetts, show that a proposed road there was supposed to be wide enough "to make it feasible to carry comfortably four oxen with four

Take Notice !

Entertainment for

GENTLEMEN AND LADIES.

At the WHITE HORSE TAVERN,

Newbury-Street,

MY friends and travellers, you'll meet
With kindly welcome, and good cheer,
And what it is, you now ſhall hear ;
A ſpacious houſe, and liquors good,
A man, who gets his livelihood,
By favours granted ; hence he'll be
Always ſmiling, always free :
A good large houſe for chaiſe or chair,
A ſtable well expoſ'd to air :
To finiſh all, and make you bleſt,
You'll have the breezes from the weſt.
And—ye, who flee th' approaching Sol,
My doors are open to your call,
Walk in—and it ſhall be my care,
T' oblige the weary traveller.
From Attleborough, Sirs, I came,
Where once I did you entertain,
And now ſhall here, as there before,
Attend you at my open door,
Obey all orders with diſpatch,
—Am, Sirs, your ſervant,

Iſrael Hatch.

Boſton, May 14, 1787.

From an old woodcut
Courtesy Walter Muir Whitehill, Boston Athenaeum

Advertisement in *The Independent Chronicle and the Universal Advertiser* under date of May 24, 1787. Israel Hatch was a widely known tavernkeeper of Attleboro, Wrentham and Boston, also at one time was a stagecoach driver, Postmaster of Attleboro and part owner of a stagecoach line for carrying mail and passengers between Providence and Boston.

barrels of cider at once." We trust that no one ever cheated by transporting any liquids stronger than cider!

One of the prime movers in the organization of the Norfolk and Bristol turnpike venture was Colonel Israel Hatch who had seen service in the Revolution but attained the rank of Colonel in the militia of later days. He was a native of Attleboro and at the outbreak of the Revolution was a stage driver over the Post Road between Boston and Providence. In 1780 he purchased the old *Garrison House* in his home town. This was the oldest tavern in Bristol County, dating from July 5, 1670, when John Woodcock was licensed "to keep an ordinary at the ten mile river (so-called) which is in the way from Rehoboth to the Bay." Hatch renamed the place "*Steamboat Hotel*" and maintained a public house there until his death in 1837. In 1789 he was appointed by President Washington the first postmaster of Attleboro and kept the office in the *Steamboat Hotel*. He apparently was a man of great vigor and enterprise as he divided his time between Attleboro and Boston where he was proprietor or manager of several busy taverns. We reproduce, through the courtesy of Walter Muir Whitehill of the Boston Athenaeum, an advertisement by Hatch when he assumed management of the *White Horse Tavern* located on the west side of Washington Street (then Newbury Street) about opposite Hayward Place. He also became the owner in 1794 of the *Hatch Tavern* in Boston on the east side of Tremont Street between West and Boylston Streets and at the beginning of the nineteenth century he was conducting the *Royal Exchange Tavern*, one of the most famous in the country, located on State Street, Boston. He also owned a tavern in Wrentham in 1798 so he was a boniface of wide experience. His son-in-law, Stephen Fuller, Jr., became proprietor of the *Half Way House* in South Walpole, said to have been built in 1807, which, of course, was patronized by the first stagecoach line to give daily service between Boston and Providence, launched about 1793 by none other than the energetic Israel Hatch.

Courtesy Federal Reserve Bank of Boston

Hon. Charles S. Hamlin and directors and officers of the Federal Reserve Bank of Boston, guests of Mr. Philip R. Allen at luncheon October 24, 1928, at Fuller's Tavern, South Walpole, leaving for Mr. Allen's home in one of the stages formerly in use on the old Boston-Providence Stage Line. Mr. Allen was a partner of Hon. Charles Sumner Bird and for many years chief executive officer of Bird & Son, Inc. of nearby East Walpole.

From an original painting in the collection of the Boston Public Library

View of Tremont Street showing the *Hatch Tavern* on the east side, between West and Boylston Streets, in front of the Haymarket Theatre

Opposite the *Half Way House*, on the east side of the highway, was the *Polley Tavern* kept by Nathaniel Polley. Both were famous for the good meals they served. Here horses were changed and time was afforded passengers for refreshment and relaxation before resuming their travels. Competition was great but business was so brisk that in due course a friendly compromise was reached whereby all stages pulled up at the tavern on the right-hand side of the road, thus giving the Boston-bound business to Polley while Fuller's tavern got the patronage of the passengers headed for Providence.

Before leaving this busy thoroughfare, it might be interesting to mention that there was a tavern in Norwood which had what was apparently a rather unusual bit of accommodation for its patrons. A large hook was placed on its front so that riders could easily toss their reins over it, thus losing no time in getting ready to have their thirst quenched. That section of the town thereby became known as "The Hook."

CHERRY TAVERN
Ponkapog, Canton, Massachusetts

WHEN THIS TAVERN, also known as *Cherry Tree* or *Cherry Hill Tavern*, began business in 1827, it was quite apropos that the signboard should bear a picture of a cherry tree with the legend "John Gerald, Cherry Tavern, 1827." Its location was on Cherry Hill which, in turn, took its name from the trees planted by John Kenney who built the original small gambrel-roofed house on the site in 1753. Kenney was active in patriotic causes during the Revolutionary period and was one of the five men to represent his town at the Congress held at the *Doty Tavern*, mentioned in our chapter on that hostelry. He was also a minuteman and a member of the Committee of Inspection. In 1778 his townsmen selected him to bear a message to General Washington and in 1783 he was elected Representative to the General Court.

The Kenney property remained in the possession of that family until 1818 when it was bought by John Gerald. In 1826 the original house was enlarged by adding another story and extending it to the west. The cherry trees which Squire Kenney had planted were now in their prime and attracted many who were fond of this fruit. Undoubtedly, possession of this natural resource was a prime inducement for Gerald to open the place as a public house a few years later. As a matter of fact, we find that in 1839 he informed his patrons that he still retained "the well-known stand called the *Cherry Tavern*, where he will continue to receive and entertain his customers with the choicest fruits and viands of the season." The fruits so advertised were no doubt the cherries for which his place was noted. He also was successful in the cultivation of strawberries for the enjoyment of his patrons.

Gerald died later that year and in 1841 the property was purchased by Francis Sturtevant who carried it on as a tavern until his death in 1863. Later, it came into the possession of Dr. Samuel Cabot of Boston after service in the Civil War. He converted it to a private residence to accommodate his numerous family and immediately installed mosquito nets on all doors and windows as he was convinced that these pests were carriers of disease. Many years later, of course, this theory was confirmed by medical scientists. At the present time the estate is owned by Mrs. Eleanor Cabot Bradley, granddaughter of Dr. Samuel Cabot, and daughter of Godfrey L. Cabot who has always taken a great interest in this property and who helped us with this chapter.

The cherry trees which brought fame and prosperity to this old tavern of Canton have been replaced by various other trees, including maple and willow. A few years ago Dr. Godfrey L. Cabot planted there seeds of the rare *Metasequoia*, known as China's "dawn redwood," a distant relative of the giant sequoia of our Pacific coast area. The seeds came to him as a gift from Dr. Elmer D. Merrill, former Director of the Arnold Arboretum, who arranged for them to be brought to Boston from China.

RARE TAVERN SIGNBOARDS

*from the interesting collection assembled by Morgan B.
Brainard, President of the Aetna Life Insurance
Company, Hartford, Connecticut.*

This rare sign hung in front of the *Wadsworth Tavern* at the junction of
Prospect Avenue and Albany Avenue in Hartford, about a block from
the present home of Morgan B. Brainard. This house is still standing,
but has been changed so that it now fronts on Prospect Avenue instead of
on the Albany Road.

Reverse Side of the Wadsworth Tavern Sign

This "Bird in the Hand" sign hung on an inn in Coventry, Connecticut.

The tavern at Saybrook Point, Connecticut, which is still standing, hung out this *Black Horse* signboard.

Sign from a tavern in Farmington, Connecticut.

This sign hung in Rocky Hill, not far from Middletown, Connecticut, in front of a tavern known as the *Yellow House*, which was conducted by Oliver and Mary Pomeroy. The initials stand for their names.

This attractively designed signboard
hung from a tavern on the Windsor
Road in Hartford, Connecticut.

This particularly interesting Bacchus
sign is supposed to have hung from
a tavern owned by the Backes family
of Norwich, Connecticut.

Temperance sign from a tavern in Colchester, Connecticut,
conducted by a man named Willard.

End of reproductions of signboards from the Brainard collection.

SOME CONNECTICUT
TAVERN STORIES

CAPTAIN ABIJAH PHELPS, the proprietor of the *Red Lion Tavern* of North Colebrook, Connecticut, had five daughters and was concerned as to how to marry them off. He therefore decided to give dances at his inn to attract beaux, and stated that soon he would bring about the desired result. He hung five bonnets along the fireplace and as each daughter procured a spouse, he said that he would take one bonnet down. Unfortunately his plan did not bear fruit, for only one daughter got married, therefore the remaining four bonnets continued to adorn the mantel, it is said, until the year 1937.

A writer of Connecticut history in speaking of inns of the earlier days described in an amusing way what a guest might hope for, but seldom found.

> Clean sheets to lie in wherein no man had been lodged since they came from the landresse, and have a servante to kindle his fire and one to pull off his boots and make them clean, and have the hoste and hostess to visit him, and to eat with the hoste or at a common table if he pleases, or eat in his chamber, commanding what meate he will according to his appetite. Yea, the kitchen being open to him to order the meat to be dressed as he liketh it best.

The last proprietor of Wadsworth Inn was a direct descendant of the Wadsworth who seized and hid the Connecticut Charter of 1662, but as for himself he did not achieve much success. His only claim to any importance seems to have been his huge size and judging from the photograph sent us by Morgan B. Brainard, space here would not permit of its reproduction.

From a charcoal drawing by the late Roy F. Heinrich
Courtesy National Life Insurance Company, Montpelier, Vermont

The "High Chair Treatment" being given at the *Green Mountain Tavern* in Bennington, Vermont. This form of punishment was used in the early days, in the same manner as the pillory and stocks, for the public humiliation of offenders.

Photographed by Vaughn Studios
Courtesy of Arthur B. Appleton, President of Beverly Historical Society

Signboard of the *Star Tavern* which formerly stood on Cabot Street in Beverly. It is now in the Beverly Historical Society. Thomas Farris, born in Manchester, Massachusetts in 1792, was at one time proprietor.

Courtesy of Mrs. Amelia E. MacSwiggan
of The Essex Institute, Salem, Mass.

This Lynnfield sign was presented to The Essex Institute, Salem, Massachusetts, in 1889 by the late David Mason Little.

Courtesy of Mrs. Howard W. Kent
Concord Antiquarian Society
Concord, Massachusetts.

Reverse side of the sign of the *Patch Tavern*, Concord, Massachusetts.

Photographed by Robert T. Rafferty.
Courtesy of Mrs. Edward S. Baker
of the Dedham Historical Society.

The proprietor made use of the species of horse known as "Cob" on his sign. Notice a faint outline of a stagecoach in the lower background. This Cobb tavern was on the road between Canton and Sharon.

Photographed by The Watson Studio.
Courtesy of Mrs. Harold G. Look
of the Haverhill Historical Society.

Signboard from *Enoch Bradley's Tavern* in Haverhill, Massachusetts, where Haverhill's heroine, Hannah Duston, spent the night of her return from captivity by the Indians.

Both sides of an interesting and curious signboard from a tavern in Portsmouth, New Hampshire.

Courtesy of Mr. and Mrs. Bertram K. Little

*Courtesy of Edwin B. Worthen,
President of the Lexington
Savings Bank.*

This tavern, kept by William Simonds from 1810 to 1828, was situated on the Old Concord Turnpike in Lexington.

*Photographed by Lynch Photo, Peabody
Courtesy of Harry E. Trask, President
of the Peabody Historical Society.*

This unique sign was found in a barn on the John Proctor homestead in Peabody in 1908 and is now in the Peabody Historical Society. Proctor was hung in 1692, a victim of the Witchcraft delusion.

Courtesy of Henry B. L. Dimmick

Sign from the *Half-Way House* in Bourne, Mass., conducted by David Dimmick about the year 1795. Henry B. L. Dimmick, who sent us the photograph reproduced, was born in this stagecoach tavern.

*Photographed by The Look Photo Service.
Courtesy of Mrs. C. M. Underhill*

From the *Ballard Tavern* of Andover, Massachusetts. A reproduction is used as the sign of the Andover Historical Society, supported by an ancient beam and crossbar, once a part of the *Blunt-Berry Tavern*.

This old swing sign until the 1880's hung in front of Moses Gragg's tavern, on Canton Avenue near the junction of Blue Hill Avenue and Brush Hill Road in Milton, known as *Blue Hill Hotel*. Teele's *History of Milton* states that it was "a famed resort for fancy dinners and high living." Gragg, previous to 1828, was joint owner with Francis Alden of the popular Norfolk Hotel (also known as Gragg's Hotel) on Court Street, Dedham, described in last year's booklet.

Reverse of Gragg sign, showing a reproduction of Blue Hill in the distance. Moses Gragg's life story, as written by himself, is owned by his great grandson, Richard H. Davis of Framingham, Massachusetts, and includes his experiences from the time he was a hostler, then tavern owner, until he moved to Milton and later to Roxbury. His friends said he kept his stable cleaner than most women keep their kitchens.

Photographed by Robert T. Rafferty
Courtesy of Mrs. Edward S. Baker of the Dedham Historical Society

The two sides of the original and attractive signboard understood
to have been in use at Bennington, Vermont, now in the collection
of the Shelburne Museum of Shelburne, Vermont, which is
described in another chapter.

Courtesy Shelburne Museum, Shelburne, Vermont

THE COMING OF THE IRON HORSE

IT IS NECESSARY to go outside of New England to find an unusual summing-up of the relative advantages of staging as compared to traveling on the "Iron Horse." This statement comes from Tony Weller, professed to be the greatest of all stage drivers on either side of the Atlantic, and who in no uncertain words makes these objections to the change from the old days, but to no avail:

> I consider that the rail is unconstitutional, and a inwader o' privileges. As to the comfort — as an old coachman I may say it — veres the comfort o' sitting in a harm-chair, a lookin' at brick walls, and heaps o' mud, never comin' to a public 'ouse, never seein' a glass o' ale, never goin' thro' a pike, never meetin' a change o' no kind (hosses or otherwise) but always comin' to a place ven you comes to vun at all, the werry picter o' the last! As to the honor and dignity o' travellin', vere can that be without a coachman, and vats the rail to sich coachmen as is sometimes forced to go by it, but a outrage and a insult! And as to the ingen, a nasty, wheezin', creakin', gaspin', puffin', bustin' monster always out o' breath, with a shiny green and gold back like a onpleasant beetle; as to the ingen as is alvays a pourin' out red-hot coals at night and black smoke in the day, the sensiblest thing it does, in my opinion, is ven there's somethin' in the vay, and it sets up that 'ere frightful scream vich seems to say, 'now 'eres two hundred and forty passengers in the werry greatest extremity o' danger, and 'eres their two hundred and forty screams in vun!

Various aspersions were quite naturally cast on the railroad by New Englanders just as the turn was taking place, doing away with the stage companies, many of the taverns, the large stables and their occupants, blacksmith forges and shops. The change came even more quickly than from the sailing ship to steam. It was claimed that most of the horses would have to be killed as they would now be useless. The late Alice Morse Earle mentions in *Stage Coach and Tavern Days* that someone declared:

There would therefore be no market for oats or hay. Hens would not lay eggs on account of the noise. It would cause insanity. There would be constant fires from the sparks from the engine. It was declared that no car could ever advance against the wind.

The *Boston Courier* in 1827 made this astonishing statement:

The project of a railroad from Boston to Albany is impracticable, as every one knows who knows the simplest rule of arithmetic, and the expense would be little less than the market value of the whole territory of Massachusetts; and which, if practicable, every person of common sense knows would be as useless as a railroad from Boston to the moon.

A stage driver, ridiculing the locomotive, offered to lay a wager that no builder could make an engine that could haul a stagecoach from Washington to Baltimore faster than his favorite team of iron grays. It was also said of him that he could leave Philadelphia on a six-horse coach, with a hot johnny-cake in his pocket, and reach Pittsburgh before it could grow cold.

From the Essex Institute Historical Collections we find in Volume XI, from the able pen of Robert S. Rantoul, the following remarks about the passing of the stagecoach:

My uncle, says the Bagman in telling the story, rested his head upon his hands and thought of the busy, bustling people who had rattled about years before in the old coaches and were now as silent and as changed. He thought of the numbers of people to whom one of those crazy, mouldering vehicles had borne, night after night, through all weathers, the anxiously expected intelligence, the eagerly looked for remittance, the promised assurance of health and safety, the sudden announcement of sickness and death. The merchant, the lover, the wife, the widow, the mother, the school-boy, the very child who tottered to the door at the postman's knock, — how they had all looked forward to the arrival of the old coach! And where were they all now!

Mary Caroline Crawford in her *Old New England Inns* gives us a parting glance at the old stages as they roll out of the picture:

No longer the host hobbles down from his rest
In the porch's cool shadows to welcome his guest
With a smile of delight and a grasp of the hand
And a glance of the eye that no heart could withstand.

> When the long rains of Autumn set in from the west
> The mirth of the landlord was broadest and best;
> And the stranger who paused over night never knew
> If the clock on the mantel struck ten or struck two.
> Oh the songs they would sing and the tales they would spin
> As they lounged in the light of the old-fashioned inn;
> But the day came at last when the stage brought no load
> To the gate as it rolled up the long dusty road.

A good many stage drivers turned to the railroads to eke out a living but it is said that they were constantly worried lest the noise and smoke would tend to injure their health.

When the trains first appeared a Boston newspaper jocosely declared that even the witches came out of their graves to see these new conveyances pass over the new railroad from Boston to Salem.

W. Outram Tristram in his *Coaching Days and Coaching Ways* has a good deal to say on this particular subject:

> Yes! Railway days and Railway ways, or rather the romance of them will not be written even when posterity has taken to balloons, for the hurry of the concern is not only fatal to romance, but is fatal to any collection of it, if any romance at any period existed; and some sort of prophetic insight into this truth, a sort of sad perception of what posterity, by its rejection of stage coaches, would be eternally bereft, breathes through the following threnody of a great coachman, of the new gods, but whose name, as Keats supposed his to be, is writ in water, or perhaps in rum and water, which would in this case be a fitter emblem of effacement.

A realistic tale is related in *The Nancy Flyer* * of a race between the fast vanishing stagecoach and the newly arrived train. In a tavern, so the story goes, someone remarked that "nobody could live for a minute agoing at such a speed." Others in favor of the railroad believed it would put many a town on the map; and again, when the country roads were heavy the smooth rail looked favorable for the railroad. This book also speaks of the excitement when the first train appeared in Littleton, New Hampshire. "Folks will get sick of these little

---

*From *The Nancy Flyer*, by Ernest Poole. Copyright, 1949. Reprinted by permission of the publishers, Thomas Y. Crowell Company, New York.

trains with such awful smoke and noise," it was said, but in spite of everything traffic continued to improve. Soon a wager of $100 was made that "The Nancy Flyer" stagecoach could beat the train on a five mile stretch near the *Bull Moose Tavern*. Everything was gotten ready for the exciting race, axles greased, harnesses gone over, and the six fastest horses prepared for the fray. On the way to the start, which was at Lisbon, New Hampshire, so the story continues, the farmers turned out to encourage the driver and his helpers, and in the meanwhile the driver was exhorting his steeds "Babies, babies, here's your pa right back of you! Show me, show me — pick her up! *Nancy* is a beggin' to go!" The anecdote continues:

> All this time, we could hear the roar of the train a coming closer. I looked back and saw the fireman stoking fast as he could chunk in wood, while the engineer yanked his throttle open wide. Louder and louder came the cheers of those who had money on the train. Closer it crept to us, neck to neck!

As the old stage forged ahead of the train the bugler came out with the very usual coach refrain — "Oh, Dear, What Can the Matter Be?" As the roar of the locomotive dropped back and died away the driver of the coach chuckled: "Iron horses!" adding to his companion, "there's something kind of pathetic to me in these newfangled railroad trains."

A grand celebration took place at the Union House of Littleton. Someone reasoned it out that the trains could take the freight but the stages would still carry the passengers in summer for the sheer joy of the rides — but such was not to be.

There also appeared in print these few lines, sad for the friends of the stages to realize, but a fitting end for this chapter:

> We hear no more the clanging hoof
> And the stage coach rattling by;
> For the steam king rules the troubled world,
> And the old pike's left to die.

STATE STREET TRUST COMPANY

MAIN OFFICE: CORNER STATE AND CONGRESS STREETS

*Ship models and old prints in an atmosphere
reminiscent of early Colonial counting houses.*

UNION TRUST OFFICE: 24 FEDERAL STREET

*Models, prints, etc., depicting the progress of avia-
tion from balloon and glider days to the present.*

STATE STREET TRUST COMPANY

MASSACHUSETTS AVENUE OFFICE:
CORNER MASSACHUSETTS AVENUE AND BOYLSTON STREETS

COPLEY SQUARE OFFICE: 587 BOYLSTON STREET

At each of our offices we have tried, by means of historical collections, to create an unusual and attractive atmosphere for those doing business with us.

STATE STREET TRUST
COMPANY
BOSTON, MASSACHUSETTS

★

*MAIN OFFICE
Corner State and Congress Streets

★

UNION TRUST OFFICE
24 Federal Street

★

*MASSACHUSETTS AVENUE OFFICE
Massachusetts Avenue and Boylston Street

★

*COPLEY SQUARE OFFICE
587 Boylston Street

★

SALES FINANCE DEPARTMENT
581 Boylston Street

★

*Night Depository Service Available

★

Member Federal Reserve System
Member Federal Deposit Insurance Corporation